P9-BIW-723

Toward a Canada-Quebec Union

Toward a Canada-Quebec Union

Philip Resnick

McGill-Queen's University Press
Montreal & Kingston • London • Buffalo

© McGill-Queen's University Press 1991
ISBN 0-7735-0864-3 (cloth)
ISBN 0-7735-0865-1 (paper)

Legal deposit second quarter 1991
Bibliothèque nationale du Québec

Printed in Canada

Publication of this book has been supported by the
Canada Council through its block grant program.

Canadian Cataloguing in Publication Data

Resnick, Philip, 1944–
Toward a Canada-Quebec union
ISBN 0-7735-0864-3 (bound)
– ISBN 0-7735-0865-1 (pbk.)
1. Canada – Politics and government – 1984–
2. Quebec (Province) – Politics and government – 1985–
I. Title.
JL27.5.R38 1991   320.971   C91-090108-2

73607

This book was typeset by Typo Litho composition inc.
in 10.5/13 Garamond.

Contents

Preface

It is the summer of 1990 – sun-drenched days and cool evening breezes, out here on the country's western periphery, far from the Atlantic seabord and first colonial outposts where it all began. Like many other English-speaking Canadians, I would like to forget about Meech Lake, the constitutional squabbles we have just been through, the intellectual and moral bankruptcy of what passes for a government in Ottawa and in a good number of the provinces. The temptation to give oneself over to the pleasures of the beach, or the summer cottage – for those lucky enough to own one – to contemplation of eagles and oyster beds, loons or sea-gulls, or to the noisy reverie of open-air cafés and music festivals is overwhelming. We have surely earned a respite from our political toils.

To summon up, even for a moment, the roller-coaster sensations caused by recent events – the blackmail from Quebec, Ottawa, and a bevy of establishment circles regarding the survival of Canada were Meech to be turned down; marathon first ministers' negotiations behind closed doors giving rise to the quasi-deal of 9 June; the slow unravelling of that deal once Mulroney's hubris in a *Globe and Mail* interview of 12 June set the stage for Elijah Harper's courageous filibuster on behalf of native people and Clyde Wells's ultimate postponement of a vote in the Newfoundland House of Assembly – is to risk ruining one's holidays.

To suggest, as I shall in the course of this essay, that our constitutional travails have only begun, that in the months and years to come English Canadians, no less than Québécois, will find themselves obliged, willy-nilly, to rethink their institutional arrangements, indeed their very identities within the existing federal state, is to risk pressing readers beyond the limits of their patience. "Give us a break," I can hear the retort, as Canadians seek to get on, innocently enough, with the routines of their daily lives.

I am no masochist, deriving perverse pleasure from dragging out constitutional discussions for the sheer hell of it. Nor do I, for one moment, think that there aren't other matters of more pressing concern at the end of the twentieth century to inhabitants of this country, let alone our planet. In an era when the globalization of capital extends to the ex-Communist world and to the whole of the ex-colonial one as well, when democratization – not always clearly defined – is on everyone's lips, when our environmental survival is put in peril by our economic greed, and when native rights have become a burning issue, it seems almost petty to be debating French-English relations and our respective nationalisms one more time.

Yet debate them we must, because in an odd way the failure of Meech Lake has set the stage for a more thoroughgoing examination of who we are and who we want to be than anything that has come before. English-speaking Canadians, in whatever region of the country they find themselves, can no longer assume that the rubric of the British North America (BNA) Act, with its monarchical trappings, less than democratic political institutions, and original division of powers between centre and provinces, will easily survive the removal of Quebec from the equation. We may be forced to address, for the first time, the type of institutional arrangements we would like to have for a government of English Canada and the core values – political, economic, social, and cultural – with which we wish these arrangements to be associated. Québécois, for their part, having mentally crossed the threshold between living in a province with a status more or less like the others and demanding for

Quebec significantly greater powers than the federal arrange-ments originating in 1867 can sustain, will also be forced to ask themselves some hard questions. What project of society do they set for themselves in these neo-liberal times, and what ongoing ties do they envisage with English-speaking Canada, if they are not to bring economic, no less than political, catastrophe down on their own heads.

So I find myself taking pen in hand, much as I did in the aftermath of the free trade election of November 1988. Then I chose the form of imaginary letters to a Québécois friend, hop-ing to make clear to Québécois readers (and perhaps to some English Canadians as well) that there was such a thing as English Canadian nationalism, no less legitimate in its own way than the nationalism that had so dominated Quebec society in recent decades. My letters earned me a venomous response from my Quebec nationalist counterpart, Daniel Latouche, and, more im-portantly, through my frequent forays into Quebec over the past year, an awareness that there could be no reconciliation of the interests of English Canada and of Quebec within the existing federal structures. Where many English Canadians looked to the federal government as the mainstay of their identity, a majority of Québécois looked just as firmly to the government of Quebec. Where English-speaking Canadians (a good half of whom today are of non-British origin) had for the most part come to terms with multiculturalism, many Québécois considered multicultur-alism a real threat. Where the Charter of Rights and Freedoms, with its notion of individual rights, has won a wide constituency in English Canada, collective rights, particularly in areas of lan-guage and culture, hold greater sway in Quebec.

In an important sense, I am less angry and less pessimistic today than I was in December 1988, when I wrote my *Letters to a Québécois Friend*. The passions that free trade brought to the surface in English Canada showed that we had our own sense of identity to assert. If Robert Bourassa and the political and business elites of Quebec were able to swing a decisive bloc of sixty-three seats into the Conservative column in the November 1988 election, if Bourassa could run roughshod over anglophone rights in Quebec the following month with his override, through Bill 178, of the Supreme Court judgment on the sign language provisions of Bill 101, it would not be without a price. Nemesis – that most Greek of goddesses – would be waiting in the wings in June 1990 to bring Bourassa's carefully constructed Meech Lake house of cards tumbling down. "Tit-for-tat," a good number of English Canadians would be tempted to say – "Quebec had its way on free trade and Bill 178; we have had ours on Meech Lake."

As for prevailing views of the future, many of those who equate the survival both of Canada and of English Canada with the continuation of existing federal arrangements may well be plunged into deep despair. I do not mock them nor doubt the sincerity that the supporters of Meech Lake in English Canada brought to their cause. But I never believed that Meech Lake, had it passed in the end, would have brought us more than a phony peace in constitutional matters. And the long-term costs – in rancour, divisiveness, and a sense of broken promises – would have made it infinitely more difficult for us to remake our relationship than may presently be the case.

As it is, we have spared ourselves unnecessary delay and joined a phalanx of other societies around the globe whose history, at the end of the twentieth century, has suddenly speeded up. We can permit ourselves the luxury of a wide-ranging debate about what English Canada is, what it aspires to become, and how we can forge a new relationship with a more autonomous Quebec. We can speak to our Québécois counterparts not as enemies, but as a people – dare I say a nation? – with interests of our own to assert. We can begin the process of moving toward a new Canada-Quebec union, knowing that we may well be setting an example for other multinational federations around the world.

This essay is written, first and foremost, for English Canadian readers interested in considering alternatives that would allow English-speaking Canada to survive and to prosper, even as its ties with Quebec become looser. But the essay, in part at least, is also addressed to Québécois readers, a majority of whom are looking for options somewhere between a familiar federalism and the full sovereignty for which only hard-core Quebec indépendantistes really strive. They may be interested in the perceptions of an English-speaking Canadian who is convinced that we must seek a new basis on which to share the northern half of this continent and a country as well.

P.R.
Vancouver
July–August 1990

Toward a Canada-Quebec Union

Why Meech Lake Failed

Was the Meech Lake Accord doomed to fail? When the agreement was first signed in June 1987, it was widely trumpeted as an act of restitution that would reintegrate Quebec into a constitution whose patriation and amendment its government had failed to support back in November 1981. Quebec's minimal conditions – its recognition as a distinct society, a decisive say on future immigration into that province, the right to opt out of federal-provincial cost-shared programs with full compensation, the right to nominate the three Supreme Court judges from that province, and a veto over future constitutional changes on matters vital to it – were met. And they represented, we were told, the most modest constitutional demands put forth by a Quebec government in decades. They seemed, all said and done, a small price to pay to make Canada symbolically one again.

True, it now comes out that there had been resistance from both Ontario and Manitoba in the behind-closed-doors negotiations that took place first at Meech Lake in April 1987 and subsequently in the Langevin Block in Ottawa in early June of that year. Concerns had been voiced about a possible weakening of federal power, about the implications for transfer payments to the poorer provinces, and about what entrenching Quebec's "distinctiveness" in the constitution might do to Charter rights. More importantly, the package unveiled on 3 June 1987 contained more than Quebec's initial five demands. It extended to all the provinces the same powers – save distinct status – that Quebec had sought, while tacking on to these the right of the provinces to nominate future Senate appointees and the entrenchment of annual first ministers' conferences on constitutional matters.

To many, in the heady days of June 1987, any objections might have seemed paltry, as the leaders of the federal political parties and provincial politicians of all stripes scrambled to get aboard. True, Pierre Elliott Trudeau, the architect of constitutional patriation in 1981 and arch-opponent of Quebec nationalism through the 1960s and 1970s and into the 1980 referendum battle, had lashed out loud and clear against an accord he saw as emasculating the federal government and setting Quebec on the road to special status. But only hard-core Trudeauites of the type that peopled the Liberal-dominated Senate seemed given to follow the musings of their old master.

The process of ratifying Meech Lake proceeded with scarcely a hurdle, beginning with the Quebec National Assembly on 23 June 1987. Within the next eighteen months the accord had been passed by the House of Commons overwhelmingly and had received approval in seven other provincial legislatures, with only a handful of legislative assembly members, here and there, voting against it. During the federal election campaign of 1988, so dominated by free trade, Meech Lake was scarcely mentioned. Few would then have predicted the constitutional storms about to erupt and bring the Canada-Quebec relationship to full crisis.

The sequel is now familiar history, and I will only sketch it briefly. Public opinion in English-speaking Canada, which had become significantly polarized by the free trade debate, was in a more nationalist mood after 21 November 1988 than at any previous time during the decade. There were many – I was one of them – who felt that Canada could not suffer the twin blows of free trade, with its opening of our economy and society to greater American influence, and Meech Lake, with its weakening of the federal government with which so much of English Canada's identity was caught up. Many who might have swallowed hard, had free trade been voted down, and accepted Meech Lake, felt little compulsion to do so knowing that Robert Bourassa, and Quebec more generally, had given Mulroney the parliamentary majority to pass a free trade agreement that had failed to secure majority approval in English Canada. A sea change in the mood of English Canadians, especially those of a liberal-left persuasion, was under way.

Even more important, I suspect, was the impact of Robert Bourassa's override of the Supreme Court ruling on the sign provisions of Bill 101. The Supreme Court, as many will recall, found that Quebec's language law, by making illegal the use of English on commercial signs in Quebec, was in violation of the federal Charter of Rights and of Quebec's own human rights code. It was prepared to acknowledge the legitimacy of Quebec's concern for the primacy of French within the province and suggested a compromise, allowing for signs with French lettering twice the size of English in areas where English was widely spoken. This was unacceptable to Quebec nationalists, who organized mass rallies in a matter of days, to denounce any significant abridgement of Bill 101. The Bourassa government then introduced Bill 178, using the notwithstanding clause of the federal Charter to override the Supreme Court judgment and maintain the prohibition on the use of English on outside signs in Quebec. The one gesture to Quebec's anglophone minority was an acceptance of English, with letters one-half the size of French, on inside signs in largely English-speaking communities.

Three of the four anglophone ministers in the Bourassa government resigned over the matter, and within months a new political party, the Equality Party, had been formed, garnering significant support from Quebec anglophones in the provincial election of September 1989 and securing four seats in the National Assembly. Outside Quebec, reaction was also swift. The newly elected minority Conservative government in Manitoba, under Gary Filmon, announced that it was withdrawing the Meech Lake resolution scheduled to be debated in the legislature. And in the months that followed, one could feel a shift in public opinion across English Canada, increasingly concerned that the distinct society provisions of Meech Lake would allow future Quebec governments to make mincemeat of minority-language rights, notwithstanding the language provisions of the Charter.

The growth of anti-French groups like the Alliance for the Preservation of English in Canada (APEC) and hostility to the extension of French-language services to various municipalities in Ontario (Sault Ste Marie, for example) and to the continuation of French-language immersion schools in localities like Sechelt, BC, were the bitter fruit of this new mood. They suggested that the bilingualism and biculturalism philosophy that had underlain federal government policy since the late 1960s, and that had come to be accepted, if at first reluctantly, in various parts of English-speaking Canada, would not easily survive the strains of linguistically rooted nationalism. To that degree, Bill 178 and the Quebec override of the Supreme Court judgment symbolized the beginning of the end of official bilingualism across the length and breadth of Canada.

Political developments in several provinces and at the federal level hastened the unravelling of Meech Lake. In New Brunswick, the Liberals swept to power in April 1988, headed by a premier, Frank McKenna, committed to important changes to the accord. In Newfoundland in 1989, Clyde Wells, a strong opponent of Meech Lake, was elected premier; he would make his views forcefully known at the first ministers' conference held in Ottawa in November 1989. A Manitoba legislative committee conducted extensive public hearings and came up with a set of all-party demands for changes to Meech, including a Canada clause, the clear precedence of the Charter over the distinct society provisions, and moves toward an elected Senate. The federal opposition leaders, Ed Broadbent and John Turner, both Meech champions, announced that they would be stepping down as leaders of their respective parties. Within both the New Democratic Party (NDP) and Liberal Party, opponents of Meech Lake rallied to candidates like Dave Barrett, Audrey McLaughlin, and Jean Chrétien.

As the three-year deadline for ratification of the Meech Lake Accord by the ten provincial legislatures approached, it became clear from surveys that opinion in English-speaking Canada had turned decisively against it. While some opponents on the right, like the National Citizens' Coalition or the Reform Party of Canada, might be seen as simply anti-French, many more, in the centre and on the left of the political spectrum, did not see themselves as opponents of Quebec or of French-language rights, but as defenders of federal powers or of the Charter. Within Quebec, conversely, Meech Lake had become a rallying point for nationalist opinion, even opinion that might have opposed it as too minimalist in 1987. Amendments of any sort to Meech Lake or the failure to pass it in English Canada would be – and indeed have been – interpreted as deep-rooted hostility to Quebec and its aspirations.

By March 1990, when the Newfoundland legislature withdrew its original support for the accord, the handwriting was on the wall. The Bourassa government, determined never to be outflanked by nationalist opinion again, was prepared to brook no changes to the letter of the original accord. English Canadian opponents were equally determined to wrest significant changes through, for example, a parallel accord or a significantly reworked package. Only a miracle of political leadership would have been able to break the deadlock.

Partisanship, locker-room humour, sleaze, an obsessive preoccupation with image – these Brian Mulroney has projected in spades, but deep principles and a statesmanlike ability to rise above the mêlée have been conspicuously absent from his repertoire. Here was an anglophone prime minister, moreover, who had come to power in 1984 determined to use Quebec nationalism to his own advantage, even while completely oblivious to the existence of another nationalism in this country, namely English Canadian. His instincts on free trade had been crassly continentalist, much like the foreign policy he had pursued. Forty percent of his caucus, after 21 November 1988, was made up of members from Quebec, and his debt to Robert Bourassa for delivering the federal Quebec vote to the Conservatives in the 1988 election knew no bounds. Could one expect such a figure, one who had underwritten the original accord by bartering away federal powers, to reconcile the forces in English Canada seeking modifications and those in Quebec opposing the slightest change?

The name of the game became one of securing all the requisite signatures on the Meech Lake document, with only verbal concessions to the dissenting provinces regarding constitutional change further down the line. The tactics employed boiled down to threatening the collapse of Canada, pure and simple, if Meech were not ratified, and getting the media and significant representatives of elite opinion on side. Through April and May and into the first weeks of June, when the first ministers finally met, Canadians were subjected to a barrage of cajolement and threats without precedent in our constitutional history.

And it almost worked. On 9 June, following a week of exhaustive behind-closed-doors discussions that ironically received massive live coverage on television, the prime minister, the premiers, cabinet ministers, and associated officials gathered for a televised signing ceremony in the National Conference Centre. The Meech Lake Accord, unaltered, would be submitted to the legislatures of Manitoba, New Brunswick, and Newfoundland, accompanied by a list of future constitutional changes to be considered – a Canada clause, Senate reform – and the written opinion of six leading constitutional experts ostensibly clarifying the relationship between the distinct society clause and the Charter. True, Premier Wells made it clear, with the asterisk beside his name, that he himself did not approve of the new package and would merely bring it back to his province for consideration either by his legislature or, if time permitted, by his electorate through referendum. And the three Manitoba leaders (Gary Filmon, Sharon Carstairs, and Gary Doer) had only granted their approval *in extremis*, convinced this was the best that could be wrested out of a tainted process. Still, on the night of 9 July and for the next few days, especially after Clyde Wells abandoned his referendum option and went for a free vote in the Newfoundland House of Assembly instead, it looked as though Mulroney, Bourassa and company would in fact get their accord. It would be difficult for the Newfoundland legislature alone to say no, and with three-party agreement in Manitoba, passage of the deal, despite procedural impediments, seemed a formality.

Enter Brian Mulroney with his *Globe and Mail* interview of 12 June, boasting about how he had rolled the dice and snookered his opponents by forcing them into a round of negotiations with the Meech Lake clock at five minutes to midnight. And enter Elijah Harper, the only native member of the Manitoba legislature, as unlikely a hero for English Canadians opposed to the accord as Premier Wells had become.

Harper, avenging centuries of neglect of native concerns, was able to stall the process by a precious week by using the requirement for unanimity to impede the quick passage of Meech through the Manitoba legislature; he then further insisted on separate debate of each different component. At the same time, 3,000 Manitobans, mostly native, had signified their wish to be heard at the committee stage of consideration of Meech, ensuring the 23 June deadline could never be met – not without total abridgement of the legislature's rules.

In Newfoundland, the soundings that provincial members of the legislature took in their ridings showed strong opposition to the accord, even as tens of thousands of telegrams and letters from across the country showed that Premier Wells reflected English Canadian opinion far more faithfully than did the eight other English Canadian premiers or the supposedly national government in Ottawa. All signs indicated that the Newfoundland legislature would vote against ratification. The last desperate

manœuvring by the federal government on 22 June, offering
Manitoba an extension on the Meech process, which Newfoundland had requested for itself but had been refused, spelled the
ignominious end of the road for the accord. The Newfoundland
House was simply adjourned without a vote.

Meech Lake may have formally died on Saturday, 23 June
1990, as the long faces of Senator Lowell Murray and Brian
Mulroney or the anguish of editorial writers and media pundits
might suggest, but it is my contention that the reasons for the
failure of Meech Lake go much deeper and must be analysed if
we are to begin to move beyond the present impasse.

Meech Lake ultimately failed because it could not bridge the
conflicting perceptions of federalism – and of Canada itself – in
English Canada and in Quebec. By opening up the Pandora's
box of constitutional change, while supposedly assuaging Quebec's demands, Meech made it inevitable that other issues –
Senate reform, aboriginal status, Charter rights – vital to other
Canadians would be raised with ever greater insistence. Just as
importantly, the accord was the product of a politically flawed
process – elitist, male-dominated, and anti-democratic to the
core – something the frenzy of media coverage only served to
underline. In a period that has witnessed moves to democratization and democratic constitution-making in Eastern Europe,
the Soviet Union, and Latin America, the top-down style of constitution-making in Canada that we inherited from our past has
lost all credibility.

If we look back at the evolution of Canada starting in 1867,
there has always been a perceptual difference of Confederation
on the part of English-speaking Canadians and French Canadians.
The identity of the former, to a significant degree, has been
caught up with and forged by the federal government in Ottawa.
When English-speaking Canadians think of nation-building, they
think back to such instruments of national policy as the tariff,
the transcontinental railways, the Mounties, or the CBC. If they
think further afield, they may summon up memories of Canadian
participation in two world wars, each of which did much to

hasten Canada's emergence as a middle power in its own right in world affairs.

These institutions or events do not reverberate with equal resonance within the French Canadian psyche. This is not to suggest that French Canadians, from the *coureurs des bois* to Georges-Étienne Cartier, Wilfrid Laurier to Henri Bourassa, Georges Vanier to Pierre Elliott Trudeau, did not make a palpable contribution to the emergence of a Canadian identity. Quite the contrary. Still, John A. Macdonald's National Policy set the stage for the take-off of what was essentially an English-controlled capitalist development, even in Quebec; the railways made possible the colonization of the West by settlers who, in the aftermath of the Riel rebellions and the Manitoba Schools Question, were to become English speakers, whatever their ethnic origins. The Mounties were too "Royal" to ever win the affection of French Canadians, while the CBC, through Radio-Canada, was to give voice to a Quebec reality, at least as much as to a Canadian, almost from its inception. As for Canada's coming of age through two world wars, nothing in this century brought the country closer to dissolution than the bitter strife between English and French Canadians over conscription and Canada's participation in European conflicts.

Even when traditional values had dominated, when church and notables ruled the parishes and politicians like Lomer Gouin, Alexandre Taschereau, or Maurice Duplessis were ensconced in office, there was an affective gulf between Quebec and the rest of Canada and significant differences in mores and social practices. French Canadians felt differently – linguistically, culturally, in the all-important religious sphere – from their English-speaking counterparts. And Quebec governments, whatever their partisan stripe, tended to be stalwart defenders of provincial autonomy against the forces of centralization or secularism threatening from without.

With the coming of the Quiet Revolution, with the wholesale modernization of Quebec's administrative apparatus, educational system, and social policies, and with the spur to a more significant French Canadian presence in the Quebec economy, the content of Quebec nationalism was significantly altered. But far from vanishing, as certain liberal adepts of modernization and technocratic transformation might have hoped, Quebec nationalism became an even more potent force in the years that followed.

Where the old Quebec political elites had been prepared to leave economic decision making to Ottawa and *les anglais* and to fund only minimal social programs at the provincial level, post-1960 Quebec governments became interventionist in the economic arena and welfare state–oriented in the social field. As a result, they competed with Ottawa when it came to spending powers and tax revenue and, more than ever before, asserted a specifically Quebec identity. Linguistic and cultural questions formed a continuing backdrop to these changes. The St-Léonard riots and protest rallies against Bill 60 in the late 1960s and wrenching debates over Bill 22 and the passage of Bill 101 in the mid-1970s led to the promulgation of French as Quebec's official language, even as the federal government was redefining Canada as a country with two official languages with rights from coast to coast. Support for out-and-out independence also grew in the 1960s and 1970s, culminating in the 40 percent "Yes" vote in favour of the Parti Québécois's 1980 referendum request for a mandate to negotiate a form of sovereignty-association with the rest of Canada.

The long reign in Ottawa of a government headed by a federalist French Canadian, Pierre Elliott Trudeau, one with massive majorities in Quebec; the 60 percent "No" vote in the 1980 referendum; adoption of the Charter and constitutional package in 1981 despite the Quebec government's opposition; the eventual defeat of the PQ in 1985 – all these might have led many in English Canada to believe that Quebec nationalism had been tamed. Nothing could have been further from the truth. Many of the proponents of the "No" side in the Quebec referendum, such as Claude Ryan or Solange Chaput-Rolland, were committed to a much more decentralized federal system than was Trudeau, if not to a form of special status for Quebec. And the Bourassa government, from December 1985 on, would pursue precisely such an objective through its initial five constitutional demands, carried over in turn into the Meech Lake Accord. At the same time, the entrepreneurs who became the much-sung heroes of Quebec in the 1980s, displacing the artists and intellectuals of two decades before, gave nationalism a new cachet. There was, therefore, by 1990, when Jean Chrétien became leader of the Liberal Party of Canada, scant support for an Ottawa-centred view of federalism in Quebec.

English Canada constitutes a more heterogeneous society than does Quebec, and it would be a mistake to assume there has been a single English Canadian perspective on federalism throughout the long post – Second World War period. Voices for strong provincial power have not been lacking, from W.A.C. Bennett to Bill Vander Zalm in British Columbia, from Ernest Manning to Peter Lougheed in Alberta, not to speak of successive Ontario premiers. And there have been issues – aboriginal rights, multiculturalism, right versus left in social policy or energy development (the multinational corporation versus the National Energy Program) – to undermine any would-be consensus.

If I may hazard a generalization, however, it is that English Canadians have a good deal more of a libidinal investment in the federal arrangements deriving from 1867 and in the larger entity we call Canada than do Québécois. It was the federal government, the old Dominion government for those of Loyalist or British descent, that was heir to the British Crown, Empire, and Imperial Government that had once ruled this country. It was to Canada – not to Quebec, Ontario, Manitoba, or British Columbia – that flocks of immigrants were to come from the late nineteenth century on. Our citizenship is Canadian; our Charter rights are Canadian; key symbols like flag, currency, passport, and laws are Canadian. Regional loyalties certainly exist, as do ethnic ties, within the larger Canadian mosaic, but rare indeed are those who believe in a sovereign British Columbia, Ontario, or Alberta.

English Canadian identity is clearly tied up with the structures and institutions of the Canadian state. Up until now, English-speaking Canadians have not been given to thinking of themselves as constituting a nation, either politically or sociologically speaking. They have lacked a catalyst to crystallize sentiment in the way that Quebec governments have tended to do for many Québécois. Nor is it easy to disentangle the sentiments of being Canadian from what is involved in being an English-speaking Canadian in particular.

Almost in reaction to nationalist sentiment in Quebec over the past three decades, however, and to the forces of North American continentalism, English Canadian nationalism has begun to emerge. It has not been hostile to Quebec's aspirations to greater self-affirmation within Canada or to a redefinition of Canada on the basis of bilingualism and biculturalism. But, inevitably, concerns have been voiced about Quebec's demands for ever greater powers in the economic or, constitutional fields vis-à-vis Ottawa and about the implications that any further decentralization of Canadian federalism would have for the rest of the country. Canadians outside Quebec are simply not willing to sacrifice their identity for Quebec nationalism.

Many British Columbians, for example, do not entertain the warm feelings toward their provincial government that so many Québécois nationalists seem to have toward theirs. On the contrary, a good number of those who lived through the nasty and polarizing neo-conservative onslaught of the early 1980s would not want to see provincial power over social policy or immigration or the judiciary enhanced by one iota. They look to Ottawa and to national institutions as significant counterweights to the often ill-conceived policies and outlandish posturing of their provincial politicians. For most, there is a sense of common political institutions, cultural references, and economic ties with fellow Canadians in other provinces. British Columbians – and

I dare say the people of Saskatchewan or Ontario or Nova Scotia – are not interested in seeing Canada transformed into a loose confederation of regions with provincial satraps in control. This is precisely what the decentralizing thrust of Meech Lake threatened to put into motion.

There is, therefore, diametric opposition between what many Québécois seem to want – recognition as a distinct society along with a much weakened federal government, at least where they are concerned – and what most English Canadians in the other nine provinces and two territories desire – a reasonably strong and cohesive central government. No poorly drafted constitutional package – which is what Meech Lake was – could paper over these differences or impose a shared vision of a country based on two quite different sociological realities. It is because the logic of English Canadian nationalism, however weakly articulated, pulled in one direction and the logic of Quebec nationalism in another that one saw, in the end, a strong majority of public opinion opposing Meech in English Canada and supporting it in Quebec. One could no more convince English Canadians that enhanced powers for all the provinces or a less than consistent application of Charter rights across the country could correspond to their preferred vision of things than one could convince Québécois that loyalty to Canada or principles like bilingualism and biculturalism could override their commitment to enhanced powers for Quebec. Is it any wonder that Meech, despite the best efforts of our consociational elites and their academic and media hangers-on, fell victim to this fatal flaw? One cannot make constitutional arrangements for one of our sociological nations while turning a blind eye to the interests of the other.

If the content of Meech was unacceptable to most English Canadians and came to be seen as doubly so in the aftermath of free trade and Bill 178, what are we to say about the process? In the early 1980s, in the aftermath of Trudeau's patriation of the Canadian constitution, a few voices had been raised in op-

position to what was seen as a high-handed, top-down proce-
dure. Mine was one. In a slim volume entitled *Parliament vs.
People*, I argued that sovereignty in a democracy worthy of the
name rested with the people, not their elected politicians, and
that constitutional documents in particular required ratification
through referendum approval if they were to meet the test of
democratic legitimacy. Another voice at the time, interestingly
enough, was that of Gil Rémillard, then a professor of constitutional law at Laval University, who was no less offended by
the lack of democracy in what had taken place: "The patriation
of the constitution of Canada and the constitutional amendments
it includes were made illegitimately ... above all, because they
do not expressly comply with the wishes of the electorate. Only
a referendum could permanently settle the question of its legitimacy."* Sitting in the seat of power, as he came to do as
Quebec's minister of intergovernmental affairs after 1985, led
Rémillard to a radical change in perspective. After all, it was *his*
constitutional package that came to be adopted in the Meech
Lake Accord. Never once, thereafter, did one hear Rémillard
speak out about the lack of popular input in the Meech process:
on the contrary, it was he, in the few short days after the 9 June
signing ceremony, who told Premier Wells that a referendum
in Newfoundland would be an impossibility where Quebec's
own constitutional timetable was concerned. So much for con-
sistency and deep democratic principles on the part of one of
the would-be architects of our constitutional future.

The Meech Lake Accord was significantly less open to popular input than had been the case with the constitutional package
of 1980–81. At least in the latter case a joint parliamentary committee had conducted public hearings that were not purely *pro
forma* and had resulted in significant amendments to the original

---

* Gil Rémillard, "Legality, Legitimacy and the Supreme Court," in Keith
Banting and Richard Simeon, eds., *And No One Cheered: Federalism, Democracy and the Constitution Act* (Toronto: Methuen, 1983), 199, 201.

proposals. And there had been significant mobilization by women's groups and aboriginal peoples in the last stages of the debate, after 5 November 1981, resulting in alterations to the Charter reflecting their concerns. Still, it was Parliament, with the assent of nine of the premiers, rather than the people of Canada as a whole, that gave the Constitution Act of 1982 the force of law – a significant denial of the notion of popular sovereignty.

With Meech, Brian Mulroney, Robert Bourassa, and others told the Canadian people in no uncertain terms that there was no room for amendments; Quebec's initial demands brooked no change. Consequently, the process of committee hearings that followed, both in Ottawa and in most of the provincial legislatures, was largely a sham. The deal had been struck behind closed doors and, if ratified, would have consecrated the process of closed-doors first ministers' conferences as the privileged venue for constitutional change for all time to come.

Somewhere between June 1987 and June 1990 it began to dawn on growing numbers of Canadians, at least English Canadians, that such a process for implementing constitutional change would simply not do. By what right – without the explicit sanction of their electors – did Brian Mulroney and the ten premiers who had signed the original accord deign to enact major constitutional changes that would affect the operation of federal institutions like the Senate and Supreme Court for decades to come, alter the balance of power between federal and provincial governments, undercut Charter rights by consecrating Quebec's distinct status, or introduce a new requirement for unanimity on future changes affecting key federal institutions? From whom does power in our system derive – the people or the politicians whom we elect every four or five years to govern over us? In the Canadian context, heavily influenced by our British past with its notions of King/Queen-in-Parliament and parliamentary sovereignty, the bias has clearly lain in favour of our elected politicians.

But this is the end of the twentieth century, not the middle of the nineteenth, and the lessons of revolutions past (the American, the French), reinforced by those of the present (Eastern Europe or Latin America engaged in the transition from authoritarianism to democracy), loom larger than might have been true in the fledgling colonies of the 1860s groping toward union and a constitution modelled on that of Great Britain. Rights, including the right of the people to have the final say in deciding by which fundamental laws they are to be governed, are perceived as perfectly common-sense principles by Canadians of our day. Why show greater deference to authority than Poles or Czechs or Balts or Russians or Argentinians or Nicaraguans who are only now regaining long-lost freedoms? Why allow Mulroney and Bourassa and Vander Zalm to hijack powers that in the end derive from the sovereign people of this country?

I do not want to overintellectualize the popular reaction or claim that the nearly 70 percent of Canadians who, according to a July 1990 *Globe and Mail*/CBC poll, found the Meech process undemocratic, had a fully worked-out notion of popular sovereignty to put in its place. Still, instinctively, if gropingly, these Canadians had come to the conclusion that constitution-making over our heads, as practised by our elites, would simply not suffice in this day and age and that a more open and participatory process was required. As offensive as any of the specific provisions of the Meech Lake Accord was the secretive process by which it had been struck and subsequent attempts to rule out any meaningful popular input. Meech Lake, thus, also failed because it had become a symbol of the monopoly of power exercised by our elected *nomenklatura* of premiers and prime ministers and of the refusal of our elites to broaden and deepen democratic practice in this country.

Two Sociological Nations

In a magazine article published in 1963, André Laurendeau asked the question, "The Anglo-Canadian Nation?" Reacting to the new nationalism then surging through Quebec, he wondered whether and when there would be a responding voice in English Canada. "It is possible to imagine that to protect itself against the troubles in Quebec, English Canada might forge a new sense of unity and learn to define itself once again. Then we would have *someone to talk to* and they could talk back, and the battle would be fierce. But that would be better, it seems to me, than messing around in the kind of swamp we are all bogged down in now."*

It is my contention that Laurendeau, in the long run, has proven a truer prophet of our dilemma in Canada than either Pierre Elliott Trudeau or René Lévesque.

Trudeau's position on federalism is known to most of us, as is his deep-rooted opposition to ethnic or tribal nationalism and, more generally, to the nationalism of the nation-state. Much of his twenty years in federal politics was spent trying to put his principles into practice and to contain Quebec nationalism within a larger multicultural ensemble. When he left office in 1984, some years after the defeat of the Quebec referendum

---

* André Laurendeau "The Anglo-Canadian Nation?" in Philip Stratford, ed. and trans., *André Laurendeau: Witness for Quebec* (Toronto: Macmillan, 1973), 243.

and the passage of his Charter of Rights, he might well have thought that his life's labour was accomplished. By the early 1990s, nothing could be less sure.

Lévesque, for his part, looked to Quebec, not Ottawa, for the fulfilment of his political dreams. More and more, from his years as a key reforming minister in Jean Lesage's "équipe du tonnerre," to his break with the Liberal Party in October 1967 to argue a sovereignty-association position, to the formation of the Parti Québécois in 1968, which he led until his withdrawal from politics in 1985, he came to incarnate Quebec nationalism. His was not the radical nationalism of the Front de libération du Québec (FLQ) or of the Rassemblement pour l'indépendance nationale (RIN), for that matter, totally intolerant of minority linguistic rights, but a Quebec nationalism, nonetheless, which looked to a sovereign Quebec with its own constitution, its own place in the concert of nations, its own army, its own economic and social policies. Yet, realist that he was, he was prepared to accept an ongoing economic association with the rest of Canada, hence the association side of the sovereignty-association formula. But little else would continue to bind the two nation-states of Canada and Quebec, once sovereignty had been secured. Lévesque died in November 1987, no doubt convinced that his dream of sovereignty had been dashed. In the early 1990s, can we be so sure?

Laurendeau never held political office (save as an opposition Bloc populaire member of the Quebec legislature back in 1944–48). Yet more than either Trudeau or Lévesque, he embodied the pull between nationalism and federalism experienced by many French Canadians. He himself had been an arch-nationalist in the 1930s and 1940s, spearheading Quebec's opposition to conscription in 1942. The newspaper that he came to edit had a long and venerable association with French Canadian nationalism, going back to Henri Bourassa. But *Le Devoir*, under his stewardship, also became the most consistent and intelligent critic of Maurice Duplessis and his corrupt regime during the years of "the great darkness." And in the 1960s, Laurendeau became the proponent of a renewed federalism, calling for a royal commission on bilingualism and biculturalism (the B & B Commission), and becoming its co-chairman from its creation in 1963 until his untimely death in June 1968.

For many English Canadians, Laurendeau's name is identified with bilingualism and biculturalism and, therefore, with the attempt to extend French-language rights across the length and breadth of Canada. Yet important as this principle may have been to him, Laurendeau was also quite unlike anti-nationalists such as Trudeau. He continued to see Quebec as a nation and to posit the need for a new political arrangement in Canada based upon the reality of two sociological nations.

For a long time, few in English Canada were prepared to heed Laurendeau's call. The final report of the B & B Commission (published in six volumes between 1967 and 1970), steered well away from addressing the question of a political restructuring of Canadian federalism of the type Laurendeau might have envisaged. Nor, over the next couple of decades, did the notion of two nations win widespread endorsement in English-speaking Canada. Rather, English Canadians, guided by federalists like Trudeau, were prone to insist that their identity sprang from a federal state called Canada, of which Quebec was an integral part, rejecting as some fanciful neologism the very term "English Canada."

Yet the time may have finally come, in the aftermath of Meech Lake and its futile attempt to reconcile the old federal structures with the specificity of Quebec nationalism, to take Laurendeau's question seriously. Is there an English Canadian nation, at least in the sociological sense in which many of us may be prepared to acknowledge the existence of a Quebec one? How might we characterize its underlying values and assumptions? Where might multiculturalism or the role of our first peoples fit into our conception of nation? What about our francophone minority, or the anglophone minority of Quebec, and the implications for any recasting of Canada in terms of two sociological nations? Who can be said to speak for English Canada?

Key attributes of nationhood usually include language, culture, shared history, geographical space, and economic links, to which may be added more subjective elements like the desire to continue to do things together as a community. Political structures may or may not exist to provide focus and direction.

A century ago, race would have figured prominently in the discourse of imperialist-minded spokespeople for an English-Canada. Yet the term "race" has been seriously tainted by the uses to which it was put in Nazi ideology, and it fits very imperfectly the mixture of peoples that could today be said to make up English-speaking Canada. Do our aboriginal people have any less claim to a constitutive part of our identity than those of British origin? Are those of south or east European origin to be seen as racially different from those of British or Nordic? Do we invent separate categories for those of Asiatic descent or East Indian or West Indian or Latin American, new and important sources of immigration to Canada, especially in recent decades? We do well, I would suggest, to limit any use of the term "English Canada" to a community of shared language and, putatively, culture, leaving notions of race and ethnic origin aside.

This does not mean that English Canadians do not have their particular origins or religious affiliations, as the case may be. Close to 50 percent may indeed trace their roots back to the British Isles, and many others to continental Europe; yet the origins of a significant section of our population today, including our native people, are non-European. Similarly, religion has indisputably marked English Canada; for a long time it was common to contrast English Canada's essential Protestantism with the Catholicism of Quebec. There was, however, from the very beginning a significant Catholic minority among English speakers – one thinks of the Irish. And with the pattern of twentieth-century migration to this country, a far greater religious diversity has come to characterize English Canada than a century ago. Moreover, we live in an increasingly secular age in which religious identity, save for a minority of the population, plays only a residual role in our daily lives. With good reason, therefore, one can highlight religious pluralism – including a percentage of the population who claim no religion – as an essential feature of contemporary English Canadian identity.

Language is the primary unifying force for English Canadians. Whatever their linguistic or ethnic origins, most of the citizens of this country, save for the francophones of Quebec and a minority of francophones outside Quebec, use English for communication. True, immigrants to Canada may live and die speaking their language of origin, which may, in turn, be transmitted to members of the next generation. But the exigencies of school system and workplace, supermarket and sporting event, mass media and voting booth, do the rest, if not for first-generation Canadians then for second. If there is, sociologically speaking, an English Canadian nation today, it is because English is its common language.

This may pose problems, when it comes to trying to differentiate us from other English-speaking countries, most especially the United States. Unlike Danes or Czechs or Iranians, we are not a national grouping with a unique claim to the use of what passes for our national language. Much as Austrians or German-speaking Swiss faced with the Germans, Walloons or Québécois faced with the French, or Argentinians or Mexicans faced with the Spanish, English Canadians must invoke cultural traits, geographical location, or political institutions to make a case for their particularity.

For all the false modesty and sense of inferiority that characterize English Canadians forced to come to terms with who they are, certain characteristics seem obvious enough. We inhabit a cold, northern habitat where harsh winters are the rule and shield, forest, and tundra predominant features of the landscape. Staple resources – fur and logs and wheat and minerals

– were for long the underpinning of our economy, and lines of communication on an east-west basis an ongoing preoccupation. Our first political institutions, inherited from Britain, were parliamentary and monarchical in character, reflecting the cautious, even counter-revolutionary frame of mind of the merchants and settlers who founded this country. To this, however, was added a federal structure suitable to what was to become a continent-wide state, a touch of agrarian and working-class radicalism in Western Canada, and, with time, liberal-democratic adjuncts like the Charter. As for culture, despite pervasive British and subsequently American influence, there is a corpus of English Canadian poetry and short stories, novels and plays, films and music, television documentaries and historical works, that brooks comparison with that produced by national groupings of comparable size. Our post-secondary educational system shows a degree of student accessibility and levels of teaching and research in various fields that can stand the test of international comparison. And yes, by the all-important criteria of economic activity, gross national product (GNP) per capita and integration into the international division of labour, English-speaking Canada is not doing badly at all.

So why is the search for national identity a perennial preoccupation of English Canadian artists and writers and intellectuals? Why does the Québécois' claim of distinctiveness cause many English Canadians to cringe with horror at the need to explore their own distinctiveness? Why, almost 125 years after Confederation, do we have an ongoing love-hate relationship with the United States, a power that has had enormous influence over us, yet whose full embrace, as in the Canada-US Free Trade Agreement, many of us fear?

English Canada as a society has been marked by its counter-revolutionary past. It emerged as the by-product of the Dominion of Canada, forged in the 1860s in the shadow of Great Britain and its empire. The one early attempt at revolution in the Canadas – the Rebellions of 1837 – was put down easily enough in

Upper Canada by force of arms and Loyalist opinion. Never again would English Canadians en masse flirt with radicalism, although Western Canadians, from the Riel rebellions to the Winnipeg General Strike to the populist movements of the 1920s and 1930s, were less reluctant to do so. Indeed, as the whole history of British North America's move toward responsible government and federal union was to show, "peace, order, and good government" were to have pride of place over competing political values. No republican infatuation with "life, liberty, and the pursuit of happiness" or "liberty, equality, and fraternity" would be tolerated by the Macdonalds and Cartiers and George Browns whom our history books venerate.

Because we lacked the dramatic break with empire that the United States came to experience, or with the *ancien régime* that France went through in 1789, we have a much weaker sense of national identity. For generations, school children in English Canada have had difficulty warming to their history, try as they may. There is little exciting about the likes of John A. Macdonald, Robert Borden, Mackenzie King, or Lester B. Pearson and only limited drama to be derived from our involvement in overseas wars. We have been spared the cataclysmic experiences of Europe and Asia in this century – mercifully enough, when we think it through. But inevitably, the dullness of our history makes for a weaker sense of shared nationhood than is the lot of the Irish or Poles or Israelis or Palestinians or Vietnamese. It gives English Canadians a certain diffidence when confronted with great powers, be it Britain in the previous century or the United States in this one. Our incomplete sense of nationhood may be coloured by the absence of a powerful founding myth.

This, in turn, explains the angst of many English Canadians confronted with the new Quebec nationalism. Quebec helped provide a little colour to the panorama of the country, a touch of "on ne sait pas quoi" to distinguish us not only from the United States, but from such sister dominions as Australia and New Zealand. It conveniently allowed English Canadians to avoid the hard task of defining themselves in terms other than those associated with the political ensemble called Canada, for no one could dispute that there was a Canadian state, duly recognized by the norms of international law. What might be in dispute was the nature of Canadian national feeling and the depth of English Canadian feeling when contrasted with that of French Canadians/Québécois.

I may be in a tiny minority, but it is my perception that the sense of being Canadian, indeed English Canadian, has developed over recent decades and may well be about to blossom forth in the 1990s. There has, until recently, been something artificial about English Canadian nationalism, something that had to be instilled from above, like maple leaf flags, Expo celebrations, and constitutional patriation. English Canadians were not wont to wear their patriotism on their sleeves – if anything, this was our claim to being different from both Americans and Québécois. Can things continue to be the same, now that our differences with Quebec over free trade, Bill 178, and Meech Lake are forcing us to define our interests far more clearly than in the past?

I am not hankering after the nationalism of Europe, which twice in this century brought that continent to war and which the most recent turn of events in central and eastern Europe, for all its positive features, threatens to reawaken. Yet paradoxically, I do find in an open nationalism – one tolerant of minorities, of political diversity, and of neighbouring nations – an element constitutive of community. We are not simply atomistic individuals born into this world to pursue our relentless ambitions in some sort of unbridled marketplace. We need roots and, in part, find those roots in the physical and psychological attributes of nationhood.

That nation, for English-speaking Canadians of my generation, is no longer bound up with Great Britain. We wish Britain no ill, but it is a foreign country pursuing its own interests in its own way, more and more caught up with Europe. Its parliamentary institutions may have marked us, although not always for the good where a more participatory democratic tradition is concerned. Its tradition of common law marked our laws, though we have recently adopted a charter of rights to make up for some of its weaknesses. Even the monarchy, for long a unifying symbol for many English Canadians, differentiating us from the Americans, has lost its usefulness. I wager that a majority of English-speaking Canadians under the age of fifty would be prepared to see Canada become a republic, with a president chosen for a fixed term by the legislators, as in Germany, Italy, or India, in place of our appointed governor general. The queen could continue as symbolic head of the Commonwealth.

As for the United States, our very proximity to that power, the degree of economic and cultural spillover we have experienced, may oddly enough have innoculated us against the possible attraction of political union. We have seen American behaviour as a hegemonial power through the years of the Cold War, the role of its Central Intelligence Agency (CIA) in destabilizing governments far and wide, the use of the US Marines from the Dominican Republic to Panama, the US military machine at work in Indo-China, and have generally not been impressed. The chauvinism of mainstream American opinion turns many of us off, while the social blight that the United States has been prepared to tolerate in the name of free enterprise – large-scale homelessness in its major cities, decrepit public hospitals and public housing, underfunded social services – serves us as a negative example. Not that Canada is a paragon of virtue when it comes to treatment of its native people or to social services or to egalitarianism across class lines. But there is a less ruggedly individualist temper to our public life, and a less militaristic bent to our foreign policy. English Canadians have shown greater ideological tolerance, within and without, than Americans, and an attachment to international organizations like the United Nations (UN) and to principles of international law and co-operation reveals much about our national character.

Only a handful of English-speaking Canadians, wherever they may live, are really interested in becoming American. Here the accumulated legacy of our own history – undramatic though it may have been – has served us well. We have tended to use the state pragmatically as an instrument of nation-building, making less of a fetish of the marketplace than our neighbours to the south. We became involved in two world wars because of the British connection, and the experience made us better able to see world affairs through eyes of our own. We have been less strident in our view of nationhood, more open to the mosaic than the melting pot.

In truth, English Canada is sociologically a remarkably diverse grouping of people, which should allow us to avoid the excessively homogenizing (and intolerant) side of ethnic nationalism. If native peoples were long a submerged part of our identity, can this still be true in a period that has seen issues of aboriginal rights and land claims posed in province after province (including Quebec) and in the territories in forceful fashion? Can it be that Elijah Harper, in helping to kill the Meech Lake Accord, did more to advance the claims of native peoples to a privileged place within the English Canadian mosaic than anything that had come before? Can one conceive of an English Canada we would be comfortable living in that did not satisfactorily resolve the question of aboriginal rights once and for all?

In a similar vein, most of us would be very uncomfortable with an ethnic (I am tempted to use the German word *volkisch*) sense of English Canada. Yes, we have a British past and a significant part of our population has British origins. Is there anything more we ought to make of these bare facts? Surely we will not have charter English Canadians (of good British stock) as opposed to the rest. Nor, for that matter, will we insist that those of other origins must pass the litmus test of three or four generations of acculturation into the British-derived stream of English Canadian culture before being considered real English Canadians. To even posit such a view of English Canada is to underline its absurdity.

The English Canada I am interested in seeing as a sociological nation, living side by side with Quebec, is an open one, where citizenship is based on common institutions and political loyalties rather than on ethnic pasts. This open English Canada is also one with a significant French Canadian minority, especially in Ontario, Manitoba, and New Brunswick. These minorities, wherever numbers warrant, will continue to have claims to educational and other governmental services in their own language, even if official bilingualism and biculturalism within English Canada becomes a thing of the past. In similar fashion, the anglophone minority of Quebec, which is linguistically and culturally at one with the population of English Canada as a whole, will need to continue to enjoy fair treatment and concomitant linguistic and cultural rights within an officially French Quebec.

I shall return to the question of linguistic minorities later. For the moment, suffice it for me to emphasize that sociological nationhood need not open the door to a closed and coercive notion of nation to which all must rigidly conform. Rather, it must reflect the way in which English-speaking Canada has developed over the past century and a quarter, its regional diversity, its multi-ethnic characteristics, the importance of its aboriginal people. English Canada has English language and culture as its constitutive features, yet in a fashion that does not simply rule out all competing forms of identity. On the contrary, it must welcome the diversity that different linguistic and ethnic groups have brought, and ask no more of its inhabitants than a willingness to adhere to the values of political pluralism and democratic citizenship that we share.

There is a real problem, however, even if one is prepared to grant the proposition that English Canada potentially constitutes a sociological nation. How does that nationality find expression politically? We know that successive Quebec governments since 1960 have advanced the claim, with varying degrees of success, that they speak for a majority of Québécois. Meech Lake would *de facto* have granted the Quebec government powers to defend Quebec's distinctiveness as a society in areas like language and culture, and any post-Meech arrangement is likely to go a good deal further. The fit between sociological and political nationhood in Quebec, despite the anglophone, allophone, and aboriginal components of its population, has been a potent one.

Who can claim to speak for English Canada in the way that Quebec governments claim to speak for Québécois? Can the sociological nation that Quebec claims to be find an English Canadian interlocutor capable of speaking in a clear, coherent voice?

One possible answer is that the very diversity of English Canada makes the notion of a single voice untenable. If geographically we mean by English Canada the nine provinces outside Quebec and the two territories, no single individual or government can purport to speak for them all. Quite aside from partisan loyalties, there are deep regional cleavages separating the Maritimes, Ontario, the Prairie provinces, British Columbia, and the North. The view of the Canadian nation has rarely been the same in Edmonton as in Toronto. Why would the removal of Quebec from the equation alter this?

When we further incorporate the perspectives that might be voiced by aboriginal peoples as opposed to those of European descent, by those who advocate a reasonably strong governmental role in economic, social, or cultural affairs and those who do not, by those wanting strong federal powers and those leaning toward stronger provincial ones, we would seem to leave the door open to endless disagreement. Laurendeau's ghost might have to wait till all eternity to find an English Canadian interlocutor.

So perhaps we in English Canada have to go the next logical step if we are to put real flesh onto the bare bones of sociological nationhood. We must seek to give it political expression, much as the Quebec government does for large currents in Quebec society who see themselves as constituting a nation. We may well need a government for English Canada.

I can imagine the *frissons* this suggestion will give unrecon-
structed federalists, determined to hold on to a vision of Canada
with Quebec a province more or less like the others – "Give
our critics a sociological toe-hold, and the whole political edifice
comes crashing down." Perhaps their forebodings are justified,
though stubborn denial of unpalatable realities will not make
our problems disappear. There is an asymmetry to our present
arrangements and pattern of constitutional debate precisely because Quebec can speak with one voice and English Canada
cannot. We, on the English Canadian side, lack a set of common
institutions that can bring us together and allow us to better
articulate our shared interests. True, there are organizations at
all levels of society that operate on an English Canada–wide
basis, from English-language radio and television networks, mag-
azines, and newspaper chains, to charities like Oxfam or CUSO
(Canadian University Services Overseas), to women's groups or
environmental movements. Cumulatively, however, these cannot
give full voice to a peculiarly English Canadian sense of nationhood. Only a common political structure can do so.

The present federal government is meant to represent the
interests of Quebec – which, more and more, sees itself as a
distinct nation sociologically – no less than those of English
Canada. For over two decades now we have had federal governments headed by prime ministers from Quebec who have
seen it as their fundamental goal to win Quebec's agreement to
a set of arrangements with which many in Quebec no longer
identify. Our recent experience with Meech Lake, in particular,
shows how dangerous it is to have a federal government more
interested in convincing English Canada to accept arrangements
that may meet Quebec demands than in coming to terms with
the English Canadian side of the equation.

Nor are English Canadians better served by their nine provincial governments. Nine may seem better than one, at first
blush. But when the premiers speak with forked tongues, as Bill
Vander Zalm did, celebrating Meech Lake one year and damning
it in a television address the next, or with contradictory philo-

sophies, as David Peterson and Clyde Wells did, we are no further ahead. There is no reason, moreover, to believe that English Canadian premiers, interested in maximizing their own leverage within the existing system, will subordinate their ambitions to some overarching sense of nation. For every Clyde Wells, there are at least three Don Gettys.

If we can somehow see our way through to actually creating a political structure at the centre that can speak for English Canada, the way may well be clear for us to sit down with Quebec and rethink our institutional arrangements. For this to happen, the political will to create an English Canadian government will have to be there in English Canada, no less than the institutional mechanisms to bring it about. We shall need a great deal of dialogue and debate over the coming months and years about our collective interests and how best to respond to the constitutional demands certain to result from the all-party committee that the Quebec National Assembly has created. Certainly, it will not be possible to make use of the existing constitutional mechanism.

Let me, therefore, suggest that sociological nationhood may well dictate a rethinking of our political categories as well. Two sociological nations, one French speaking, one English speaking – if that is indeed what Quebec and English Canada are to be – may spell two political entities engaged in quite a different relationship with one another. It will require some new and hard thinking about bilingualism, about federalism, and about democratic forms of constitution-making – themes I set out to explore in the remainder of this essay.

3

Bilingualism and Its Discontents

Language is at the core of identity for many national groupings. It is through language that members of a particular society communicate with one another and come to experience their shared history and traditions. A language may be unique to members of a particular grouping or shared widely across national frontiers. Either way, it serves to demarcate different branches of humankind, no less surely than climate, religion, or territory.

French has been an integral part of French Canadian identity, though not its sole defining characteristic, going back to the seventeenth-century foundation of New France. Catholicism was the colony's official religion, and for a long time thereafter – until the secularization inaugurated by industrial transformation, urbanization, and the institutional reforms of the Quiet Revolution – it was at least as important as language in cementing French Canadian society together. Legal codes and agrarian vocation also played their part, as did the collective memory of the Conquest and of battles – political, legal, existential – fought to keep this fragment of French language and culture in North America alive.

As French Canadians dispersed across North America in the latter part of the nineteenth century, seeking economic opportunity in the textile mills of New England or the agricultural or resource-extraction communities of Ontario or the West, language would prove an ephemeral tie. Most had little choice but to adapt to a situation where English dominated the whole nexus of human relations. Religion was of limited help in stemming the tide of assimilation. Only where numbers were significant or ties possible with Quebec, as along the New Brunswick or Ontario borders, did French survive beyond one or two generations.

Within Quebec, helped by very high birth rates promoted both by agrarianism and Catholicism, French Canadians could do better than hold on. French Canadian control over education, social institutions, and civil law, for example, could preserve a good deal of the cultural values of the past and maintain the status of French as a living and evolving language. Even in Quebec, however, control over the economy slipped out of French Canadian hands with the coming of English merchants and fur traders in the late eighteenth century. Nor did Quebec governments, once Quebec had become a province with a French Canadian majority in 1867, undertake major economic initiatives to promote French Canadian entrepreneurship. The language of the workplace – at least at the senior, managerial levels – was largely English down to the 1960s.

The other side of the story also needs to be told. For the British colonists and settlers in the Maritimes, Lower Canada, and Upper Canada, English was as constitutive of identity as French for the French Canadians. The former had the signal advantages of having the post-1759 colonial power on their side and the English-speaking American republic to the south: the survival of their language was never in doubt. But English bred its own set of associations and cultural references, with religion – largely Protestant – doing the rest.

There was little that was bilingual about the Dominion of Canada established in 1867, save for the Parliament of Canada, the legislature of Quebec, and certain federal and Quebec courts. Not only was English the language of public administration for most practical purposes at the federal level, but it was also the language of instruction in schools, of work, of provincial and community affairs, the length and breadth of Canada outside Quebec. Concessions to French speakers were minimal and subject to swift cancellation; witness the Manitoba and Ontario school controversies of the 1890s and 1910s. Nor was there any shortage of members of the Orange lodges dreaming of the wholesale assimilation of the French Canadians in Quebec and the assertion of the unalloyed Britishness of Canada as a whole.

The Orangemen may have failed in this, just as they failed to stem the tide of non-British immigration into Canada in this century. But the threat they had posed and a more general fear of assimilation by anglophones continued to haunt French Canadians, fostering the cult of *la survivance*. And on the English Canadian side, animosity to the French fact as destructive of cultural and political unity would not lack for adherents, especially in periods of crisis like the two world wars.

I know this may not be the fashionable way of recounting Canadian history. Those of us who have bought into the rhetoric of the two founding peoples are expected to play down elements of tension between English and French Canadians that may have been there in the past. We are to emphasize the spirit of live and let live that underlay the Canadian experience, the ability of French Canadian leaders such as Wilfrid Laurier or Louis St. Laurent and English Canadian ones such as Mackenzie King to overcome the hurdles posed by language and culture and allow French and English alike to develop in the spirit of a common Canadianness. We are not to take the ravings of Tory hotheads in Ontario or the West or of the Abbé Groulx in Quebec, with his unrelenting appeal to race, at face value. We have supposedly learned to tame these atavistic sides of human nature.

The adoption of a federal program on bilingualism and biculturalism in the late 1960s, which brought about significant expansion of the use of French in the federal civil service and improved access to French-language services for francophones across the country, was to put paid to the old anti-French attitudes in English Canada. And on the French Canadian side, it was meant to undercut, once and for all, fears of assimilation and give Québécois better reasons to identify with the structures of the Canadian federal state. In view of the fact that religion had ceased to be a divisive factor, as in the days when ultra-montanism in Quebec and anti-papist fervour in English Canada ran deep, and that Quebec was making the transition to capitalist modernity and aligning both governmental institutions and social practices with the prevailing Canadian and North American norms, our peaceful coexistence within the federal system would presumably be easier.

But not everyone bought into the philosophy of linguistic togetherness. There were angry outbursts by separatists at some of the public hearings of the Royal Commission on Bilingualism and Biculturalism in Quebec. And anger was to swell into a storm as Quebec nationalists, in the late 1960s and into the 1970s, fought for an end to English-language education for immigrants to Quebec and for French as the language of work and communication, indeed as the sole official language of Quebec. In English Canada, the extension of radio and television services by Radio-Canada to Toronto or Calgary or Vancouver did not pass without protest, any more than did the introduction of compulsory packaging in the two languages, from toothpaste to cornflakes, or the new thrust for second-language training for unilingual anglophones in the federal civil service. These opponents of the new philosophy may only have been rednecks; the quiet majority, we were led to believe, would come to accept the virtues of a bilingual and bicultural definition of Canada.

And this a majority of English Canadians came to do. Reluctantly at first, but with less reluctance subsequently, middle-class anglophones flocked to enrol their children in French-immersion schools. English Canadians, after some initial grumbling, accepted the extra costs that the introduction of bilingualism into the federal civil service entailed and found the French fact of some value in helping to differentiate Canada from the United States. Even the notion of *la francophonie* to parallel Canada's long-established ties with the Commonwealth added a useful dimension to our foreign policy. We would show the world at large that a federal state with two major linguistic communities could transcend the petty differences of the past.

There was nothing ignoble about the objectives that the Official Languages Act of 1969 and the Trudeau government set out to advance. They were a good deal more favourable to minorities than a philosophy based on French unilingualism in Quebec and English unilingualism in the rest of Canada was likely to prove. Neither Switzerland with its predominantly unilingual cantons nor Belgium with its bitterly hostile Flemish and Walloons, separated by a language boundary down the middle (save for Brussels), seemed much of a model. And what we have seen more recently in the Soviet Union, by way of bloodshed and ethnic conflict in the southern republics, now that the iron hand of Moscow has been lifted, makes other alternatives infinitely worse.

The problem with bilingualism and biculturalism as an integral solution to Canada's linguistic and cultural differences has been its failure to address the root problem of two sociological nations. One of these nations, it so happens, feels the need for special powers to resist the potential encroachment of the other. To treat English and French on an equal footing – as the Official Languages Act and the language provisions of the Charter tend to do – was to fail to address the greater vulnerability of the French language in Quebec, let alone outside Quebec, than that of the English language. The case for special powers made by Quebec francophones of all stripes, from independentist to quasi-federalist, seemed unassailable.

Yet, conversely, to give French in Quebec special protection through laws like Bill 101 or Bill 178 appeared to many anglophones to violate the principle of reciprocity. It was all very well for Quebec to point to sins of omission and commission where the treatment of the francophone minorities outside Quebec was concerned. In part, at least, bilingualism and biculturalism represented an attempt to reverse this process, something which, as noted, a majority of anglophones outside Quebec had come to accept with time. For Quebec to play light with Charter principles, as the December 1988 override of the Supreme Court judgment indicated, was to risk dissipating overnight the goodwill toward bilingualism in the rest of Canada. English-speaking Canadians would see in Quebec's denial of the right to use English on outside signs anywhere in that province a powerful symbol of discrimination against their own language, and would react with much the same indignation as their French-speaking counterparts had when faced with any overt attack on theirs.

There had, in any case, been a certain amount of wishful thinking behind the bilingualism and biculturalism philosophy. It tended to underestimate the centrality of language to the new Quebec nationalism in a period when religion had lost its hold. Students and others were prepared to take to the streets and engage in pitched battles for the primacy of French in the educational system and throughout society. The French fact was at the heart of Quebec's identity, to be protected, cherished, and advanced at all costs. The cause of French might gain from its promotion as an official language in the rest of Canada, but the price could not be acceptance of equal status for English within Quebec. Nor could it mean choosing Canada over Quebec as the prime focus of francophone identity. If this is what lay behind the bilingualism and biculturalism exercise, as Québécois nationalists feared, they were not interested.

Proponents of bilingualism and biculturalism may also have hoped that bilingualism would become the rule rather than the exception, at least where younger Canadians were concerned. Countless resources were poured into immersion language training, exchanges between secondary school students from English Canada and from Quebec, and so on. Twenty years later we need to ask ourselves some hard questions. How many of the products of French-immersion schools in English Canada are fluently bilingual? What percentage of seventeen- to eighteen-year-old anglophones overall have more than a halting knowledge of French? How many have a feel for social, cultural, or political currents in Quebec? How many young Québécois francophones of the same age group have complete fluency in English? How many have a feel for what makes English Canada the type of society that it is? The answers, I am afraid, are a lot less encouraging than the adepts of bilingualism might have hoped.

Young English Canadians and young Québécois, even when they do have some inkling of the language of the other, have not necessarily grown closer together. They may share dress codes, taste in music, career aspirations, concern for the environment – there is, after all, a homogeneity of values at work, not only in Canada, but across the advanced capitalist world at large – but group sentiments tend to be articulated locally, not globally, and ties that bind are most often forged with those one has gone to school with, lived next door to, or worked beside. For most Québécois that means fellow francophones; for most English-speaking Canadians elsewhere in Canada, fellow anglophones.

Biculturalism further implied, if only at the symbolic level, an English-French duality to Canada that did not fully correspond to the facts. Even in the 1960s, let alone today, English Canada was culturally more diverse than the notion of a founding people of British stock would allow. Aboriginals had little place in the bilingualism and biculturalism conception of Canada, and Canadians of neither British nor French origin, despite the royal commission's grudging nod to multiculturalism, shared a place somewhere beside the stove or the wood shack. Quebec in the 1990s is also a good deal more multicultural than *pure laine* nationalists of the Lise Payette or Gilles Vigneault persuasion seem prepared to accept. Allophones, aboriginals, not to speak of anglophones, continue to dot the landscape of a Quebec that will never be purely French Canadian in character. To privilege the British and French as founding peoples, therefore, over everyone else was to risk provoking resentment.

The two groups that stood to gain the most from bilingualism and biculturalism, had it been applied uncompromisingly, were, as I have suggested, Quebec anglophones and francophones outside Quebec. As minorities living within the territory peopled by a majority from the other linguistic community, they were particularly vulnerable to discriminatory treatment. Acknowledging this fact and entrenching corresponding minority rights seemed a pragmatic, even generous, Canadian response to issues often dealt with brutally elsewhere.

Have things really worked out as well for minorities as they might have hoped? The apparatus of the federal government, including the Official Languages Commission and, more recently, the Charter, has been relatively ineffectual in stemming the pressures toward unilingualism in Quebec. It did help secure some victories against clauses in Bill 101 that denied English equal status with French in the Quebec legislature, the courts, or statutes; but the larger battle, as the Bourassa government's override of the Supreme Court judgment on signs would suggest, has been going against anglophones. Outside Quebec, the funding of French-language education services, radio and television facilities, and community centres has been more fulsome than at any time in the past. Yet the long-term survival of francophone communities outside Quebec is as problematic as ever, and francophones remain vulnerable to an anti-Quebec backlash whenever relations between English Canada and Quebec take a turn for the worse. Bilingualism and biculturalism is a doctrine for fair-weather conditions and reasonably tolerant clienteles; when conditions turn foul and zealots in each camp start attacking the language and culture of the other, it is the first casualty.

I write this as someone who is himself fluently bilingual and very much a francophile by temperament. I was born and lived my first twenty years in Quebec, spending several years, thereafter, as a student in France; on occasions too numerous to count, I have since revisited Quebec – sometimes for lengthy stays.

There is something very attractive about knowing two (or more) languages, about being able to understand and function in a culture other than one's own. It broadens the horizons and would seem to better prepare us for a world where cross-national integration is increasingly displacing the nation-state of old.

Yet the assertion of Quebec's sociological nationhood is the direction toward which political currents have been swirling for the past three decades. That assertion and the corresponding emergence of some form of English Canadian nation cannot but have telling consequences. The logic of Quebec nationalism militates more and more in favour of special powers for Quebec over language and culture and a definition of Quebec as a society with French as the sole official language. Such a vision is diametrically opposed to the spirit that underlay the original bilingualism and biculturalism philosophy.

On the anglophone side, I can scarcely conceive of English Canada maintaining the elaborate structure of two official languages if Quebec, for most purposes, ceases to be bound by common language provisions. Good samaritanism on such a scale is in short supply in the world at large and is not to be expected from English Canadians, many of whom will feel bitter and resentful over the wrenching political readjustment Quebec will now be forcing on us all.

This does not mean that in those areas where English Canadians and Québécois may continue to be joined together – for example, in the institutions of the Canada-Quebec Union that I sketch below – official bilingualism will not be maintained. Nor need it, nor should it, mean open season for attacks on linguistic minorities, either in Quebec or in English Canada – nothing would more quickly unleash blood hatred upon this land. But a future English Canada will be no more officially bilingual than a future Quebec, and the status of French within its borders will be much like that of English within Quebec – that is, the language of a tolerated minority. The principle of territoriality will come to dictate language policy in this country, for better or for worse.

My own personal conviction is that this is a less inspiring language philosophy than the one that the B & B Commission set out to foster; but it is more realistic. Language minorities on each side will pay the psychological costs of the new arrangements into which our two sociological majorities – English Canadians outside Quebec, francophones within Quebec – will be entering. English Canada will lose something as well, the putatively French side of the Canadian identity. And French itself – and here I side with Trudeau and other federalists of his persuasion against the sirens of sovereignty-association and even of special status for Quebec – will pay a high price outside Quebec for the reinforced security Quebec francophones will now enjoy within their small enclave. How many anglophones in Winnipeg or Vancouver will be interested in learning French as a second language or in sending their children to immersion language schools a decade from now? French is, after all, on the defensive in the late twentieth century, even within Europe. Why not turn to German or Spanish or Japanese or Chinese just as quickly if we are to have second-language training in English Canada? If official unilingualism and distinct society status is the road down which Robert Bourassa and Claude Ryan and Solange Chaput-Rolland and Lucien Bouchard and Jacques Parizeau want to go in unison, so be it. English Canadians, however well disposed to French as one of Canada's two official languages today, can only take note of the new Quebec reality. We will have to get on with working out our own national and linguistic priorities, in which French will not have a significant place.

Two sociological nations, each with its own official language. The demise of official bilingualism, except at the yet to be devised confederal level. A fond farewell, by some at least, to the vision of a bilingual Canada and the wellsprings of Enlightenment principles that seemed to give it birth.

– 4 –

Has Canadian Federalism Had Its Day?

Bilingualism is not the only bone of contention between anglophones and francophones in Canada. English Canadians, by and large, have identified with federal institutions and seen these as engendering national loyalties that transcend those to region or to province. A majority of Quebec francophones have resisted too close an identification between their identity and the federal state. They have, at various time, placed loyalty to province higher than have most English Canadians, arguing for as decentralized a federal system as possible, for special status for Quebec, or for Quebec sovereignty.

This dichotomy is, no doubt, too simple, since it seems to overlook the experience of a century and a quarter in which a majority of French Canadians seemed no less content with the existing federal-provincial distribution of powers than their English Canadian counterparts. It also risks overdoing the strictly federal pole of English Canadian identity, since loyalty to province or region, on the part of aggrieved wheat farmers in the 1920s and 1930s or Alberta- or BC-based resource-sector entrepreneurs since the 1950s, for example, could outweigh loyalty to a distant, central government.

Still, we do need to address the potential difference in perspective between English-speaking Canadians and francophone Québécois. One way of exploring this is through the device of ideal-types. We do not have to suppose that every English-speaking Canadian since Confederation times has necessarily aspired to a strong federal government or every French Canadian to its opposite. But we can ask ourselves whether the general tendency among English-speaking Canadians, be it in times of economic expansion like the opening of the West or times of hardship like the Depression, in periods of war or under peace-time conditions, has been to welcome or reject a strong federal government role. In the same vein, we can ask ourselves what the corresponding tendency has been in Quebec. We may also want to assess just how much more explicit such ideal-type thinking may have become in our own day, when the politics of nationalism, both Québécois and Canadian, has assumed a new vigour.

For English-speaking Canadians, the sense of nationhood was intimately tied up with Confederation. There was no Canada – and therefore no possibility of a Canadian or English Canadian consciousness – in the pre-1867 period. What one had, at best, were colonies in the Maritimes and central Canada, separated by a formidable land barrier, whose populations had only in common their status as British colonials. Governmental structures were underdeveloped, public finance in great difficulty, and the possibility of undertaking major infrastructural projects severely constrained. The quality of political life on the small stage of the colonial assemblies was not one to whet ambitions or stir the imagination.

If one of the purposes behind Confederation was purely defensive – to ward off any incipient threat from a North newly triumphant in the American Civil War – another was more positive in character. It was to lay the basis for more concerted economic activity by government, for continent-wide expansion north of the Great Lakes, across the prairies and to the Pacific, and for the forging of a new nationality. The Dominion of Canada, to which was given the lion's share of developmental powers under the BNA Act, would represent for most English-speaking Canadians and future immigrants to this country the entity with which national sentiment would be associated. The Canadian government underwrote the grants and loans with which major railway construction could be undertaken; it purchased the Hudson's Bay Company lands and erected tariff walls behind which industrialization could be pursued; it promoted immigration and policed the Northwest. The prestige of the British monarchy, through the office of the governor general, was attached to the national government in Ottawa. Canadians began to look to debates in the federal Parliament or on the hustings for milestones in their national life. Trade relations with the United States, the regulation of industrial conflict, freight rates, tariffs, commissions of inquiry into all aspects of the economy and society, naval expenditures, or the mobilization of resources, human and physical, in times of war are some examples drawn from the first half century after Confederation. The federal government was laying the basis for a sense of national identity among English-speaking Canadians.

Not everything was an emanation of the federal government, by a long shot. Provincial governments were also engaged in significant public ventures (e.g., Ontario Hydro or Prairie utility companies) or in the provision of education. Most economic activities were generated quite autonomously by capitalists and labourers, prairie farmers, or small-town businessmen. The churches and other voluntary organizations played an important role in community life. So a sense of nationhood also sprang from below, from the multifaceted activities of a civil society coming into being. The federal government, however, provided the all-important mould.

That mould would continue to shape English Canadian consciousness in the decades that followed. War, both in 1914–18 and again in 1939–45, brought home questions of sovereignty and national identity in very pointed form. It provoked deep divisions between French Canadians, largely isolationist in outlook, and English-speaking Canadians still moved by ties of blood to the old mother country. It fostered a growing differentiation between Canadian and British sentiment on the battlefields of Europe and in the diplomatic councils of the powers:

those who bled and died at Vimy or Dieppe did so as Canadians, and Canada would accede to a seat, both in the League of Nations and the United Nations, and begin to enunciate a foreign policy of its own. War also led to a strengthening of federal power – over finance, economic resources, industrial relations, social policy, and much besides – that was to have permanent consequences in peacetime.

English-speaking Canadians came to look to Ottawa as their national government in time of crisis. They came, more generally, to look to Ottawa for universal social programs, such as old age pensions, unemployment insurance, family allowances, or employment equity; for cultural initiatives, such as the creation of the CBC, the National Film Board, or the Canada Council; for the Keynesian thrust to fiscal and monetary policy that set in after 1945. They took to heart the 1956 pipeline debate, the Bomarc missile crisis of 1962–63, the Canadian flag debate of 1965, the question of foreign ownership at the end of the 1960s, constitutional patriation and introduction of the Charter in the early 1980s, free trade in 1988. Their political consciousness reflected, in good part, the nationalizing influence of federal politics.

The English Canadian sense of nationhood, therefore, has a good deal to do with the activities of the Canadian government. That government was responsible for the settling of the West; it has been asked to help stabilize the workings of the market system; it has, through social and industrial programs, helped mediate class conflict or prevent discrimination; it has provided important cultural instruments and projected our image as a people abroad. There has been a symbiotic relationship between state and nation in English Canada – to weaken the central government is, for many, to threaten Canadian identity itself.

Again, let me qualify the argument, lest I be accused of smuggling a centralizing, almost Jacobin, concept of the state into this analysis. Identities are formed by more than governments and, in a federal system, by more than the federal government alone. Provincial boundaries and regional economies engender their own solidarities, and public opinion may well side with the provincial, as opposed to federal, pole on a whole range of issues. Significant initiatives with national implications have been taken at the provincial level over the years, from the Workmen's Compensation Act in Ontario to votes for women in Alberta to medicare in Saskatchewan. Many of the issues that shape our lives, moreover – economic, environmental, scientific, social, and cultural – are ones over which governments, federal no less than provincial, have only limited control or on which citizens must take direct initiatives. We are not, fortunately, the subjects of a Leviathan or Moloch state.

Yet the federal government, for most English Canadians, is not something alien. Ideally it should retain the ability to take initiatives in a whole range of fields and ensure national standards and citizenship rights for all Canadians. In no way should it be subordinated to the particular wills of the provinces. Most English Canadians do not buy into attempts, neo-conservative in origin, to redefine Canada as some loose confederation of regions, or community of communities. Intuitively, they sense that their deepest loyalty is to a country, indeed a nation, and that a reasonably strong central government is the *sine qua non* for its continuation.

This identification with the federal government has, if anything, strenghtened over the past couple of decades. English Canadian nationalists of the 1960s, for example, looked to Ottawa for measures to reverse the inflow of foreign capital and the high degree of American control over cultural, no less than economic, institutions. The Canadian Development Corporation, the Foreign Investment Review Agency, and the ending of tax exemptions for the Canadian editions of *Time* and *Reader's Digest* were offshoots of this belief. In the early 1980s, a majority of English Canadians supported the introduction of a charter of rights that gave all Canadians, irrespective of region, language, or ethnic background, claims against their governments. It did not escape the attention of women's groups, native people, or civil libertarians that the strongest resistance to a codified charter had come from provincial governments. In the late 1980s, the free trade initiative brought home to large numbers of English Canadians the danger of aligning the country too closely with the United States. Those concerned about preserving a distinct Canadian identity on the North American continent worried about the erosion of federal powers with regard to social programs, regional equalization programs, energy initiatives, and culture. Some of these same concerns surfaced in criticisms of the Meech Lake Accord throughout English Canada. For many of its opponents, Meech was little more than a power grab by the provinces at the expense of a federal government bereft of national vision.

English Canadians may be less passionate in their nationalism than Québécois, but they know full well that their own history of coming to national consciousness has been closely linked with the federal government created in 1867. They may be open to pragmatic arguments about the efficacy of provincial versus federal power in any particular domain and to a degree of power-sharing between the two levels of government. That, after all, is the essence of a flexible federal system. They are not, however, amenable to a wholesale dilution of federal power, whatever popular sentiment in Quebec may argue. Indeed, rather than ceding this point, they would probably prefer a wholly different set of arrangements with Quebec, one that would preserve the type of federalism within English Canada that they have known.

Perceptions in Quebec have been very different, never more so than today. Georges Étienne Cartier, at the time of Confederation, may have talked about the creation of a new nationality with reference to the Dominion, but there was never to be a complete merging of French Canadian and English Canadian sentiment in this regard. For French Canadians, the sense of nation went back through the Patriote Rebellion and the post-

Conquest period to New France. Language, religion, and civil law separated French Canadians from the English who settled in Quebec after the Conquest and with whom they found themselves forced to cohabit thereafter. Confederation had one great attraction for French Canadians – it undid the forced union of Upper and Lower Canada, thereby lessening, by establishing a province of Quebec in which French Canadians were a clear majority, the danger of assimilation, which Lord Durham's report had advocated. The BNA Act for French Canadians was a pragmatic arrangement in which English Canadian merchants and settlers (and behind them the imperial government) got the central government they wanted, and French Canadians, control over education, property, and civil law in the one province that mattered to them.

This does not mean that French Canadians en bloc would never feel any affinity with the federal institutions of the new Dominion. The accession of Laurier to the prime ministership in 1896, despite opposition from the ultramontanist clergy in Quebec, could not but gratify French Canadian pride. The continuing importance of Quebec to the forging of majority governments in Ottawa, especially majority Liberal governments, would be used to good effect throughout the twentieth century. The arrangement ensured that Quebec interests would seldom be overlooked and that the division of powers set out in sections 91 and 92 of the BNA Act would generally be respected by the English majority.

Flashpoints between French and English Canadians were not lacking through the first hundred years. French Canadians perceived themselves, invariably, as getting the short end of the stick. Louis Riel was hung in 1885 over the strong objection of Quebec opinion. Manitoba revoked French-language school instruction in the early 1890s, and Ottawa could do nothing to restore it. English Canada got to build frigates for the British navy in the years preceding the First World War and, more importantly still, secured Canada's entry into that war and, in

1917, over Quebec's bitter objections, full-scale conscription. The Union government elected in December of that year showed that a united English Canada, committed to its version of nationalism, could easily overwhelm national sentiment in Quebec. During the Second World War, despite Mackenzie King's pledge not to impose conscription for overseas service, the pressure of English Canadian opinion led to the plebiscite of 1942. While 72 percent in Quebec may have voted against conscription, English Canada voted overwhelmingly in favour, forcing the federal government to finally introduce it in the autumn of 1944. In the immediate post-war years, despite Louis St. Laurent's prime ministership, tensions with Quebec were not allayed. The provincial government presided over by Duplessis resisted federal funding for post-secondary education, which had been recommended by the Massey Commission, and the greater economic and social intervention practised by the federal government overall. The fleur de lys flag with royalist blue colours adopted by the Quebec government in 1948 underlined a quite distinct sense of national past.

One must again be careful not to overgeneralize. The potted version of Quebec history presented in the Parti Québécois's white paper on sovereignty-association of November 1979 implies an unbroken tradition of nationalist resistance to the evils of Canadian federalism. Nationalist opinion has certainly not been lacking – from Henri Bourassa and the Ligue nationale of the early part of the century, to clerically inspired groupings of the 1920s and 1930s, to the Bloc populaire of 1942, or, at moments, to the Union nationale. Quebec governments, however, were not always at dagger's edge with Ottawa, nor did a significant segment of French Canadian opinion throughout this period aspire to anything resembling sovereignty or independence. French Canadians opposed English Canada's infatuation with Britain and Empire, and they simultaneously wanted a federal system in which Ottawa would scrupulously respect Quebec's jurisdiction under the BNA Act. They were certainly much less inclined to identity with the federal level of government than English Canadians, but reflecting the values of a still traditional society, they did not favour too strong a role for the Quebec government either. Theirs was essentially a defensive sort of nationalism *within* the federal system.

Let us, however, get on to the contemporary period. Events have speeded up, leading to a more radical change in attitudes. The crucial transformation heralded by the Quiet Revolution was the emergence of a modernizing (and secular) form of nationalism, at first associated with the new middle class and looking to a much enhanced role for the Quebec government. "L'état du Québec" entered the political lexicon, as did the term "québécois," replacing the long-familiar "canadien" or "canadien français." Somewhere during the 1960s, a significant number of Quebec francophones, especially of the younger generation, made a clean psychological break with the Canadian pole of their identity. They ceased believing in Quebec's place within existing federal institutions altogether. And Quebec governments, more and more, followed their lead.

From that point on, federal governments could not allay Quebec's demands. Various concessions on tax points or pension plans or representation at international conferences only seemed to whet the appetite for more. Trudeau, once he had come to power, could try hold the line and point to significant popular support for his position in Quebec. But the politics of language had a dynamic all its own, and a party committed to Quebec sovereignty came to power in 1976. Canada survived the PQ's victory and the 1980 referendum – but barely. The 40 percent "Yes" vote for the sovereignty-association option represented close to 50 percent of Quebec's francophones. A fair number of those supporting the "No" side were committed to a revamped federalism of the type the Quebec Liberal Party had proposed in its beige paper of January 1980. That paper had talked about Quebec as a distinct society and advocated much enhanced powers for Quebec along with a new federal council, named by the provincial governments, to replace the federal Senate. There is a direct filiation between some of these proposals and the ones that underlay the Meech Lake Accord.

Even so-called federalists in Quebec like Robert Bourassa were, by September 1989, openly calling for *un fédéralisme rentable* – a federalism that pays. There was no room in such a schema for a federal government, or provinces, with interests that might override Quebec's. Still less was there a place for a concept of nationhood linked to a strong federal, as opposed to a strong Quebec, state. Inevitably, such a vision would collide with that widely held by English Canadians.

I am neither censorious nor disapproving of Quebec nationalism for having come of age. It is no less legitimate for francophones in Quebec to see themselves as Québécois than it is for anglophones in the rest of Canada (and in Quebec for that matter) to see themselves as Canadians. If Quebec is sociologically a nation, as I am among the first to concede, then its people are free to articulate the concept of nationhood that best suits them. That is precisely what has been happening over the past thirty years, despite the best efforts of Trudeau and others to stem the nationalist tide.

The emergence of this new Quebec nationalism, however, has made Canadian federalism as we have known it until now unworkable. It pits a view that favours as weak a federal government as possible (or none whatsoever) against the sentiment of most English Canadians, who want a reasonably strong federal state. The nationalism of English Canada ever since 1867, as I have argued, is inseparable from the very level of government that Robert Bourassa and Gil Rémillard, not to speak of Lucien Bouchard or Jacques Parizeau, seek to undermine. There can be no federal arrangements when one of the parties insists on holding all the important cards in its own hands while failing to take the interests of the other into account. That, I'm afraid, is what the Quebec-Canada relationship increasingly has become.

We, in English Canada, need to have the courage of our convictions and stop asking Quebec for concessions it will never make. Forty percent of the Quebec electorate, going by the provincial election results of September 1989, want out of Canada (or Canadian federalism) altogether; a significant part of the 50 percent who voted for Bourassa's Liberals want the minimal possible commitment to Canada compatible with Quebec's own aspirations. These latter would include Quebec control over immigration, communications, social services, and probably the very framework of rights. Quebec's constitutional demands are open-ended, much like the term "distinct society" in the ill-fated Meech Lake Accord.

A majority of Québécois are dissatisfied with the existing federal arrangement. And if I dare say so, a growing number of English-speaking Canadians are coming to the realization that it is in our interest as English Canadians to stop trying to appease Quebec or bind it to arrangements that it rejects. Québécois want greater autonomy; we want a federal government that can articulate a sense of nationhood, which for us can only mean a Canadian nation. We need a government with the financial, constitutional, and political resources to carry such a mandate through. That government can no longer be one that includes members of Parliament or ministers from Quebec whose loyalty, à la Lucien Bouchard, is only to Quebec. English Canadians must have their own parliament and government.

Once we have mentally crossed this bridge, we too can bid farewell to the existing federal arrangements. We are opening the door to potentially significant institutional alterations within English Canada, for example, with respect to the Senate, to the distribution of powers between centre and provinces, to the formulation of Charter rights. We need to tackle the subject of ongoing relations with Quebec and engage in tough bargaining, far tougher than has been possible in our stymied constitutional deliberations until now. And we, of course, will have to continue to deal with the powerful American presence to our south.

Is Sovereignty-Association
a Viable Alternative?

Once we start thinking in terms of alternative arrangements between (English) Canada and Quebec, several possibilities come to mind. The most frequently touted has been the nation-state model, in which both Quebec and what would presumably be called Canada (minus Quebec) begin to function as fully sovereign states in their relations with one another and with the outside world. All the assets and liabilities currently vested in the government of Canada would be divided up between the two successor states, with Quebec assuming control of federal assets on its territory and a share, proportionate to its population, of the national debt. The Quebec portion of the St. Lawrence Seaway would come under its control, as would the Quebec-based assets of all federal crown corporations (e.g., CBC, Canadian National (CN), Petro-Canada). There would be a Quebec military, taking over the installations of the Canadian Armed Forces in the province; a Quebec diplomatic corps to staff its embassies abroad, including a Quebec mission to the United Nations; Quebec citizenship and passports – in short, all the accoutrements that come with sovereignty. And Canada (minus Quebec) would maintain its armed forces and diplomatic missions, issue passports, and certify citizenship as a separate, sovereign state. Quebec's National Assembly would combine the powers presently vested in the federal and Quebec governments under the Canadian constitution, exercising the legislative function for an independent Quebec; the Quebec cabinet, headed by a prime minister or president, as remains to be determined, would exercise full executive power; and the judicial system, entirely controlled within Quebec, would culminate in some type of Quebec supreme court.

This is the model that the Parti Québécois essentially put forward in its 1973 manifesto, *Quand nous serons vraiment chez nous*, and again in its 1979 proposal, *Quebec-Canada: A New Deal*, which set the stage for the May 1980 referendum. The PQ, however, was prepared to put a little bit of water into its wine where economic arrangements were concerned. Recognizing the dislocation that would be caused to the Quebec economy, and for that matter the Canadian, especially Ontario's, by a complete rupture of trading ties, it proposed the establishment of a Canada-Quebec common market, with the governments of Canada and Quebec as equal partners. The PQ was also prepared to countenance a common currency for the two successor states, with Quebec – in its one departure from absolute parity in its relations with Canada – naming only a minority of the directors to a common bank. Sovereignty-association was the name given to this amalgam.

There was (and still is) a great deal of confusion about just what sovereignty-association might mean. At the time of the Quebec referendum, for example, survey data showed that a significant portion of the Quebec electorate thought that Quebec would continue to send members of Parliament to Ottawa under such an arrangement. Nothing could have been further from the truth. More recently, the PQ has dropped the association demand from the party's platform, calling instead for sovereignty, pure and simple. Meanwhile, Quebec public opinion, reacting to the demise of Meech Lake, seems to have embraced sovereignty-association to the tune of 2 to 1 or 3 to 1, if recent polls are to be believed. But is a common market that includes currency arrangements between a sovereign Canada and a sovereign Quebec a viable proposition? And is it sovereignty that a majority in Quebec is supporting, as opposed to significantly greater autonomy for Quebec?

For political scientists, sovereignty is not some throwaway term with variable meanings. Its roots go back to the world of absolute monarchy in which one individual could claim supreme power over his or her subjects on the basis of hereditary transmission, religious sanction, or brute conquest. The term helped, moreover, to differentiate one state from another; each exercised sovereignty within its own borders without interference from an outside power. For political theorists like Jean Bodin and Thomas Hobbes, the existence of such a sovereign power within the state was the supreme good; for theorists of international relations like Hugo Grotius or Samuel Pufendorf, it was the basis on which a new international order could be built.

From the mid-seventeenth century on, however, sovereignty ceased to be the exclusive preserve of monarchs. First, the Levellers, during the English Civil War, articulated the notion of an Agreement of the People that would bind legislatures and rulers to first principles agreed to by the people. Then, in the run-up to the Glorious Revolution of 1688, liberal theorists like John Locke introduced the notion of the consent of subjects as a check on what king or parliament could do. In the eighteenth century, French philosophers railed against absolute monarchy, and the great iconoclast Jean-Jacques Rousseau, in his *Social Contract*, grounded sovereignty in the people alone. Popular sovereignty was to take off from that point on, finding expression in the declarations and constitutional documents of both the American and French revolutions.

The exercise of sovereignty, however, cannot be divorced from a state structure. And in a world more and more divided up into nation-states, there cannot be multiple sovereignties within a single state. There can certainly be a separation of powers – of the type that Montesquieu described, for example, among executive, legislature, and judiciary – but there can be only one sovereign state for purposes of international law. The Americans could help pioneer the idea of a federal division of powers, but subunits of a federation do not exercise sovereignty in the international arena. Their attempts to do so, through secession, for example, can result in bloody civil wars or in the creation of new states out of old units (as in the breakup of the Austro-Hungarian or Russian empires at the end of the First World War or of the European colonial empires in the aftermath of the Second World War).

The point of this seeming disgression is that sovereignty has cardinal implications both within the state and internationally. To say that the people of Canada are sovereign means in the end that all legitimate authority derives from them; to say sovereignty rests with King/Queen-in-Parliament, as our constitutional texts would suggest, is to ground sovereignty somewhere else. To aspire to sovereignty for Quebec is to wish that Quebec exercise all the powers in the international arena currently exercised by the Canadian state; it can mean nothing less. True, this sovereign Quebec could then decide, of its own free will, to delegate part of this sovereignty – say over economic matters – to a body made up of its representatives and those of Canada. In much the same way, states enter into treaties and alliances that pool their resources and diminish their sovereignty in some particular respect.

What is unacceptable, however, is any attempt to fudge what is at stake. A sovereign Quebec means one that has cut its links to Canada and made good its claim to represent exclusively the six and a half million or so people on its territory for domestic and international purposes. It is not a Quebec that is partly in Canada and partly out; it is not a more autonomous Quebec; it is an independent Quebec. And it asks the rest of Canada – with which it has been bound up until now – and the international community to recognize its independence.

One constant in majority English Canadian attitudes – at least on the political left and centre – to the new Quebec nationalism of recent decades has been an unwillingness to consider using force to keep Quebec within Confederation against its will – not, at least, when that will finds democratic expression through majority support in something like a referendum. Why force Québécois to be our co-citizens if their deepest inclinations lie elsewhere? There was, to put it mildly, insufficient consultation of the population of the British colonies when Confederation was originally conceived. Confederation was imposed from above, to no small degree, by politicians and the Colonial Office and has always suffered from a lack of democratic legitimacy. If the people of Quebec today wish to define themselves collectively as sovereign vis-à-vis the people of Canada and to vest that sovereignty in institutions and an elected government all their own, they have every democratic right to do so. And many of us would want no part of an English Canada that says no to them.

This much said, a sovereign Quebec would have no claims to special treatment from a sovereign (English) Canada. We would have to negotiate a fair division of assets and liabilities between our two successor states, not without very hard bargaining on each side, one imagines. The question of boundaries might be raised – Quebec hotheads dreaming of redrawing the boundary of Labrador (part of a province presided over by the hated Clyde Wells) and of annexing Acadie; English Canadian hotheads demanding that a sovereign Quebec be held to Quebec's borders of 1867 or perhaps that the west end of the Island of Montreal, largely anglophone, be somehow attached to English Canada (one can see it already, now that West Berlin has vanished, West Montreal with a wall skirting University Avenue and Mount Royal and cutting across to Ile Laval!). All this would raise the political temperature considerably and spread much ill will. Even if we surmount this – separation of physical assets, psychological rupture, moving-vans with refugees from Westmount and Nôtre Dame-de-Grace (NDG) with tales of horror reaching English Canada, Franco-Albertains or Manitobains arriving in Quebec with their own tales of woe – what would the outcome be? An English Canada well disposed to reaching economic agreements with a Quebec that has just removed itself from the Canadian body politic? A Quebec eager to forge associations with a truculent English Canada? Marital separations leave deep wounds. Why would the breakup of a country leave less?

Suddenly, the scenario of sovereignty *cum* association becomes a lot less convincing. There may be enough at stake in the trading relationship between Quebec and Ontario, let us say, to suggest that nothing overt would be done to disrupt it. Tariff walls, which are coming down around the world and within North America, are not about to spring up around Quebec. It would serve the interests of neither side. The St Lawrence Seaway, spanning Quebec, Canada, and the United States, would continue to be administered through some joint body. Air, road, and rail links to and fro would, no doubt, be maintained. Telephone and fax and postal service would continue to operate between our two states.

But would there be a disposition for much more than this, especially in English Canada? Why, for one moment, would we be interested in sharing a currency and reserve bank with a sovereign Quebec? Why would we want any Quebec input into our own monetary policy, exchange rates, interest rates, decisions about our degree of indebtedness to foreign lenders? And why would we want to take any responsibility for the consequences of economic policies Quebec governments might pursue? This would violate our sovereignty in a very fundamental way.

As for future co-operation in matters of foreign policy (as is increasingly the case with the European Community), the environment, or defence, the will would simply not be there. A sovereign Canada would be inclined to turn its back on a sovereign Quebec and, in the short run at least, to reduce any joint endeavours to the minimum. There is no point underestimating the deep sense of hurt – and therefore resentment – that would colour Canadian attitudes toward Quebec in the aftermath of separation.

So perhaps the PQ was being realistic in scrapping the association plank from its party platform a few years back. Parizeau realizes that a sovereign Quebec can hardly hitch its wagon to an English Canada from which it has just freed itself. And there is, of course, the United States – the great white knight for Péquistes from René Lévesque to Bernard Landry and for Quebec's new entrepreneurs, who have proven themselves the true heirs and beneficiaries of the Quiet Revolution. Bombardier and Lavalin and the Banque Nationale and the Groupe Laurentienne may find in the United States a power, economic no less than political, to counterbalance that of a now hostile English Canada.

And assume such a role the United States certainly could. But at what cost for Quebec and its hard-won sovereignty? Would a one-on-one relationship with the United States really serve Quebec's interests? How well would Quebec popular culture fare, inundated as it already is by American music, films, videos, and television? How well will its much-vaunted entrepreneurs measure up against the gnomes of Wall Street or the sharks of Dallas? (Robert Campeau's fall surely carries some lessons.) Will Quebec have the means of projecting its image on the present world stage, where there are many more-pressing concerns around than the arrival of one more sovereign state? Quebec's sovereignty might quickly turn out to be dross.

Let me suggest that the severing of sovereignty from association, as the PQ, for one, now proposes, will not solve Quebec's problems. It will simply underline the enormous risks Quebec would be forced to take in creating its own currency and managing its own debt, in cutting its own deals within the continental and global trading system, or in looking to the United States or further afield for the ties it will have forfeited in English Canada. Sovereignty does not come cheap. And it is sovereignty, not sovereignty-association, that Québécois will be forced to choose if they wish to pursue the nation-state model.

There is, however, a quite different option that suggests itself once one abandons the hard language of sovereignty and the spurious language of sovereignty-association. That option is a significantly looser arrangement between English Canada and Quebec under which Quebec, without becoming a sovereign state, ceases to be a province in many areas of federal jurisdiction. Quebec would continue to be linked to English Canada in ways that still need to be spelled out for purposes of foreign policy, defence, trade, currency, environment, and citizenship at the minimum. We would remain one unit for purposes of international law and external sovereignty. We would have some form of common parliament and government in those areas of responsibility that we would share. I call this option a Canada-Quebec Union.

Why might English Canadians be prepared to consider such an arrangement when they would balk at entering into an association with a sovereign Quebec and when they turned down the seemingly more limited demands contained in Meech Lake? There are at least three reasons that come to mind.

First, English Canadian nationalism is not only tied up historically with the structures of the federal state; it is, more profoundly yet, bound up with the geographical territory that Canada occupies in the northern part of North America. Quebec is a key piece of that territory, and symbolically, its removal, through its accession to sovereignty, would shatter the physical unity of that space. Quebec sovereignty would immediately raise the spectre of Pakistanization, with Canada splintered between the Maritimes and Ontario. While it is one thing to conceive of two sociological nations, English Canada and Quebec, each less than fully sovereign, forging a new relationship with one another, it is quite another to think of an English Canadian state forging such ties with a sovereign Quebec. English Canadians are simply not prepared for such a quantum leap.

Second, there was a logic to the English Canadian refusal during the debate over Meech Lake to accept a weakening of the central government where English Canada was concerned, or to acknowledge some sort of special status for Quebec within our present constitution. One could not have Quebec members of Parliament or Quebec federal ministers taking part in decisions that affected the rest of Canada when Quebec might be exempted under the distinct society provisions of Meech Lake from their application. A very different situation arises once one grants the proposition that Quebec is no longer a province like the others while ensuring at the same time that Quebec no longer has a stranglehold over the internal English Canadian agenda. In other words, English Canadians may well be willing to grant Quebec powers under a significantly looser confederal arrangement that they would not grant it within the existing federal system. Yet for any such alternative arrangement to appeal to English Canada, there must be more that unites our two nations than the exclusively economic ties that sovereignty-association implies.

Third, the advent of two separate nation-states would weaken us both when it comes to dealing with the United States. English Canada and Quebec will be tempted to play off against each other, and energies that might otherwise flow into bolstering what makes each of us unique, will instead go into currying favour with the colossus to the south. English Canadians and Québécois are not obliged to love each other, but we are condemned, by our very proximity to the United States, to curb any desire we might have to go it entirely alone.

The conclusion one can draw is the complete reverse of what indépendantistes would argue. We need an association between English Canada and Quebec far more than either of us needs sovereignty. Quebec may well want out of the existing federal system, and English Canada may find it in its own interest to negotiate a new arrangement with this new Quebec. But a Quebec that insists on sovereignty-association ensures itself the enmity of English Canada and a sovereignty (largely without association) that it may be the first to rue.

– 6 –

The American Danger

Every country has its share of myths and national stereotypes. For Canada, the United States is more than just a looming presence: it is the mythic power at our door. The United States is the source of much that is good: federal arrangements, industrial prowess, cultural brashness, technological innovation, democratic experimentation. And it is simultaneously everything that we most fear: manifest destiny, the arrogance of power, cultural imperialism, corporate capitalism in tooth and claw, liberty not always respected by those who most loudly trumpet her name. At one level, there is "the longest unguarded border in the world," the free intermingling of two peoples, economic flows and cultural ties that have made Canada as unmistakably North American as the United States, despite a more European touch to our political culture. At another, there is a fear of America's very power – whether experienced as threats of political annexation during our first half century, or of economic takeover subsequently, or as an all-pervasive presence in our cultural lives.

This is no place to begin to explore the conflicting visions of the United States that run through Canadian history. I think it sufficient to underline a dualism – fascination and attraction on the one hand, fear and trembling on the other. Usually the first has won out. But at moments, the second comes to the fore – the Fenian raids, the Alaska Panhandle dispute, the reciprocity election of 1911, the threatened extension of American network broadcasting into Canada in the early 1930s, the heights of American Cold War brinkmanship or intolerance (e.g., the hounding to death of Herbert Norman), the extension of American extra-territoriality laws to subsidiaries north of the border, control by AFL-CIO unions over their Canadian affiliates, bilateral defence agreements like NORAD with their accompanying nuclear strategy of Bomarcs and cruise missile tests, the controversy over acid rain, and most recently that over free trade. One can overdo the conflict, though the temptation to go to the other extreme and use syrupy rhetoric to celebrate an unsullied Canadian-American relationship is significantly greater – especially on state occasions.

Worth underlining as well, since it has implications for our present situation, is a significant divergence between French Canadian and English Canadian attitudes toward the United States. Confederation, one might think, would have served the interests of our two sociological nations in allowing Canada to develop as a sovereign state. Variations of such an argument surfaced in the Confederation debates and in speeches by federal politicians, especially from Quebec, thereafter. The flip side of the coin, however, is a strong attraction to the United States, going back to the lure that American republicanism held for French Canadian nationalists like the Patriotes of the 1830s, at war with the Family Compact. (I, for one, can hardly blame them for that!) This attraction was subsequently to take a new form as English Canadian nationalism of the Tory variety defined itself ever more stridently in relationship to Britain. If, to English Canadians, to be a Canadian meant unswerving allegiance to British imperialism and all its works, there was a countervailing tendency at work among French Canadians. Hewing to a more isolationist position, they defined themselves as geographically, no less than psychologically, removed from Britain and its entanglements. In this, they resembled the United States, given, for reasons of its own, to turning its back on Europe. The United States also provided an important outlet for a surplus French Canadian population at the end of the nineteenth century; it provided, too, a major source of investment capital for Quebec. Americans seemed to be less haughty than the anglophones of Montreal's St James Street or Westmount, let alone Westminster; moreover, they were not interested in imposing Loyalist, monarchical values on French Canadians.

Even when English Canada began to shift its loyalties away from Britain in the aftermath of two world wars, something of the old French Canadian suspicion lingered. Canadian Tories seemed to resist subtle changes like the phasing out of the term "Dominion" in the early 1950s, to defend British actions in places like Suez, to mount trench warfare in defence of the Red Ensign with its Union Jack in opposition to the maple leaf flag, and this as late as 1965. By then, in any case, the Quiet Revolution was in full swing and the priority of Quebec governments and nationalist opinion lay in diminishing the powers of Ottawa.

Consequently, when a new Canadian nationalism emerged in the late 1960s, seeking to diminish Canadian dependence on the United States in economic and cultural matters, foreign policy and defence, it would not find allies easily in Quebec. To the degree that this new Canadian nationalism looked to the federal government to provide national leadership, Quebec nationalists were generally ill-disposed. To the degree that it might voice specifically English Canadian concerns about social or cultural distinctiveness on the North American continent, no one in Quebec was paying the slightest attention. Language and culture seemed to provide Quebec with an invulnerability that English Canada lacked. There was scant recognition of the fact that English Canada might provide a shield against Quebec's own possible Americanization or that French language and culture had survived within a sovereign Canada even as French Canadians in New England or Cajuns in Louisiana had succumbed to the American way. For nationalists, Quebec's survival seemed in no way bound up with that of English Canada, and the United States no great threat to Quebec itself. There was thus a direct linkage to an earlier type of thinking.

Let me leave Quebec for the moment and return to English Canada. On the question of the United States, there is a sharp difference of opinion, as the results of the 1988 federal election would underline. The supposed economic attraction of free trade won the Conservatives about 40 percent of the vote in English-speaking Canada, with several percent more going to formations like the Reform Party that were also in support; some 55 percent plus of the vote went to parties opposing free trade, who gave voice to English Canadian concerns about social policy, culture, and sovereignty. On a regional basis, Alberta was the one English Canadian province that strongly favoured free trade; everywhere else, a majority was on the other side. Big business favoured the arrangement almost to a man (there are not too many women in its ranks), orchestrating a huge advertising campaign on its behalf; trade unions and social movements of all sorts were in the opposite camp. What could have seemed clearer?

The real cleavage, however, runs down the English Canadian psyche and characterizes those on both sides of the free trade dispute. Economically, the ties that bind us in our external trade and capital flows and patterns of industrialization have been overwhelmingly American for at least a century; free trade accentuates this, but in doing so seems to follow the logic of geography and the trend to regionalization within the global economy. The defeat of the Canada-us Free Trade Agreement would not in itself have altered the forces at work, as even opponents of free trade would have to admit. Yet resistance to the American presence is at the heart of the Canadian experience going back to the nineteenth century. Small countries (population-wise, at least) have reasons to fear their larger neighbours. And there is a whole gamut of reasons – from counter-revolutionary in the nineteenth century to social democratic today, from strictly defensive to culturally more assertive, from the realm of foreign policy to that of basic political institutions – to keep a certain distance between our two societies. Even the staunchest supporters of free trade must have felt some trepidation on this score.

This unease has been a permanent fixture of our national existence. Events over the last number of years, however, suggest that the balance is in danger of tilting in the direction of greater American influence. The free trade agreement, now that it is in effect, has accentuated the north-south pull on our economy at the expense of the east-west one. One of the things this is bringing – I see signs of it happening already – is greater allegiance to region and a corresponding weakening of nation. Premiers like Bill Vander Zalm or Don Getty and regional economic actors will be the first to play the cost-benefit game of federalism within English Canada – "What's in it for us?" – and to demand a significant loosening in the fabric of Confederation. Will regional balkanization be one of the permanent legacies of greater continental integration?

No less dangerous is a potential anaesthetizing of the mind as Canadians come, more and more, to accept as natural and inevitable market norms or social priorities that the United States comes to adopt. We have already internalized a great deal of American cultural habits without thinking about it twice. Perhaps we will no longer be aware that we have slipped into an American mould as we seek to make our universities more instrumental and market-oriented, our notion of balance in broadcasting ever more favourable to corporate values ("Forests are Forever" ads are fine, but environmental ones are not), or our legislation on abortion one that panders to the narrow credo of the American fundamentalist right.

Our preoccupation with and differences with Quebec, moreover, as I suggested in chapter 5, can only play into American hands. So much emphasis may have to be placed on simply holding English Canada together that we may have to settle for the lowest-common-denominator definition of what Canada is – a formally sovereign state, perhaps, but little more. Or in our effort to upstage Quebec or prevent it from upstaging us, we will each be currying maximum favour in Washington or New York, whatever the costs. It will become quite impossible to manœuvre outside of an American strait-jacket or to withstand the pressure for further far-ranging concessions.

English Canadians, therefore, have to think long and hard about their historical experience and about the sacrifices that may have to be made to preserve more than the political shell of a country. Do we give free rein to those forces of regionalism within English Canada that will seek to maximize any advantage they can derive from a permanent weakening of central authority? Do we allow American values – already powerfully strengthened through free trade – to shape the very consciousness of who we are? Are there ways of bringing Quebec on side in an endeavour to preserve our *two* distinct societies, each faced with the challenge of the United States?

I have no problem with region as one pole of identity. It is only reasonable that people living on Vancouver Island or in northern Saskatchewan or Cape Breton have a different sense of place from those in southern Ontario. Most of our daily activities are rooted in the place we live. To appropriate the slogan environmentalists have been advancing in recent years, we need to think globally and act locally. There is a lot to be said for focusing on activities in one's own community or province in the real world of political behaviour.

One can go one step further, as good internationalists might do, arguing that the nation-state, indeed the nation itself, is an impediment to the type of co-operation that must take place across national borders. The hole in the ozone layer or nuclear contamination does not respect frontiers; more and more, we think of human rights as being universal in character. Why perpetuate forms of national consciousness?

I think the global dimension is a crucial part of our consciousness as we approach the end of the millennium. A host of questions, from environmental protection and economic distribution to the maximization of democracy and the extension of human rights, needs to be addressed in such terms. Still, the nation-state is not about to vanish (events in the Soviet Union suggest we may see more, not less, of them in the not-too-distant future), nor is world government about to usher in an Age of Isaiah, with lions and lambs gambolling together. We are a long way from that and must continue to use the rubric of the nation-state as best we can, even while trying to build a more co-operative, egalitarian, and, hopefully, peaceful world order.

In short, we must take the question of nationhood seriously. The United States, moreover, the power beside which we live, is little inclined to yield much when it comes to the flexing of its military muscle or the advancement of its own position in trade negotiations or the effusive (and frankly sickening) celebration of national flag and anthem. The Québécois, as we have surely learned these past thirty years, have made of nationalism something of a civic religion. We need emulate neither, but it will simply not do for English Canadians to look to either region or planet as the sole source of identity.

A structural problem, however, arises when it comes to formulating the sense of nationhood. As long as we give premiers and provincial governments a near monopoly over constitutional debate, as is presently the case, we will end up with region-oriented definitions of what English Canada is all about. Provincial boundaries take on world-historical importance, and short-term profitability for regionally based economic actors assumes a role that drowns out more far-reaching concerns. Social policies, aboriginal claims, women's rights, and any long-term balancing off of growth with environment are prone to get lost in the shuffle, and our horizons as citizens likely to be narrowly constricted as well.

We must find ways of mobilizing the sentiments of being members of a national community that lie just below the surface in English Canada. These sentiments arise from our own collective experience of nation-building and have been coloured, in part, by our fending off the American presence. The sense of danger is significantly heightened at the moment as a result of the free trade agreement and of Quebec's insistent rejection of existing federal arrangements. We are at a crossroads.

Crisis can bring its own opportunities. We need citizen movements that begin to debate and articulate the vision of a nation, and this in each and every region and province of English Canada. We need to bring together Canadians of diverse ethnic and social backgrounds. Universities and, more especially, student councils may have a crucial role to play in the process, but so do a host of organizations, from women's groups to members of our cultural community, environmental organizations, trade unions, business associations, aboriginal peoples, and ethnic groups. We need grass-roots participation in the process, for what is at stake is the kind of Canada we may be living in five or ten years down the line, with the United States continuing to cast its long shadow.

Let us have no illusions about it. The United States may have lost the uncontested hegemony that it exercised over the non-Communist world in the three decades after the Second World War. Both Europe and Japan have emerged as rival economic poles, while newer centres of activity in Asia and Latin America are beginning to stake out their claims; the ending of the Cold War has reduced some of the strategic importance of American military power; and regional conflicts (e.g., in the Middle East) are beyond easy control by the great powers. Still, American military power can be deployed across thousands of miles, as the Gulf Crisis shows. The United States remains the single most powerful economy in today's world, with extraordinary technological capability and scientific innovation at its command and with financial and corporate clout that few can rival. Within the Western Hemisphere and the North American continent, in particular, it is uncontestably the dominant power and will continue to be so into the indefinite future.

English-speaking Canadians have known this for a long time, and much of our political and economic decision making over the years has been directed to trying to manage so unequal a relationship. We have had to pay the price by accepting the role of American junior partner through the long period of the Cold War or by countenancing a degree of foreign (i.e., American) ownership over our economy for many decades that no other advanced capitalist country would have allowed. But we have simultaneously been able to develop and maintain a cultural identity of our own, establish political institutions that suit our own purposes, foster social programs like family allowances or medicare or regional equalization, and succeed in being internationally competitive in sectors from banking to agriculture, telecommunications to engineering.

But we cannot afford to go to sleep at the wheel. The United States does not threaten us with direct takeover – even if a small minority of English Canadians (and perhaps a larger number of Americans) might favour political union. The threat has always been more subtle, or, if one prefers, more insidious, since it has been expressed through cultural forms or modes of economic behaviour that Canadians, often quite unreflectingly, have assimilated. The world of the 1990s is no different in this respect from the one we are leaving behind, and the pressure for conformity, in economic matters for example, can only sharpen as free trade takes hold. Can we continue to use the state as a countervailing power to that of corporate capital, Canadian or foreign, when the "free market" – read the power of the economically strongest – is the free trade agreement's major premise? Can we pursue tax policies that are modestly progressive when the United States is determined to use its tax system to redistribute wealth to the very rich? Can Canadian trade unions hold out for reasonable safety standards or gender equality or fully vested pensions when their American counterparts have seen the unionized share of the American labour force decline to barely 15 percent today?

If push comes to shove, we may find ourselves several years down the road wanting to renegotiate the Canada-us Free Trade

Agreement in certain important respects or, if the Americans are unwilling to budge, abrogate it altogether. Will the political will to do so be there in English Canada? How much value would we place on the ability to pursue political, economic, or social objectives of our own? How strong a will would there be to resist pressure for new concessions, for example, on water, which is in short supply throughout the American West, or on our cultural industries, which are still too protected from the American point of view? We will certainly not be looking to the Business Council on National Issues to sound the alarm.

The possible development of a full-blown North American free trade agreement including Mexico may introduce yet a new variable into the discussion. At one level, it may make it more difficult for Canadians to head off the continentalizing influence of market forces; yet at another, it may give us a potential ally, Mexico, no less concerned in maintaining domestic control over key resources, such as petroleum, or in preserving its political and cultural identity vis-à-vis the United States than we are likely to be.

This leads me back to the question of Quebec and our quite different perceptions of the United States. At first blush, nothing would seem more futile than to project ahead to greater co-operation between English Canada and Quebec in this regard. Do we not owe passage of the Canada-us Free Trade Agreement to the unstinting support shown it by Quebec's political, economic, and mass media elites? Is Robert Bourassa – or any likely successor as premier of a Quebec concerned with affirming Quebec's powers against the rest of Canada – about to take the so-called American danger to Quebec seriously? Does Quebec public opinion, so heavily influenced by its own big business entrepreneurs or by pq-style nationalism, offer much of an opening in this regard?

It would be foolish for us in English Canada to appeal to Quebec on the basis of sentiment or emotion. Indeed, as I have implied on several occasions in this essay, the time for such appeals is long past. Relations between our two nations will, from now on, be conducted on the basis of hard bargaining and self-interest. This is the only language that Quebec's elites, in particular, understand and the one with which we should address them.

We in English Canada have reasons to fear too great an American encroachment on our society. We will try, as forthrightly as we can, to maintain what is distinctive about our culture, our political institutions, our social fabric, through thick and thin, whether Quebec becomes sovereign or not. But let us be frank. There are centrifugal forces in English Canada – the regionalism to which I referred – that could destroy us. Some Canadians may want to yield to the temptation of joining up with the greatest single power in the world today, one with which we share a community of language and culture. There is no absolute certainty that English Canada will survive.

Quebec's own survival is its own affair. Québécois may, however, want to ask themselves whether the continued existence of English Canada – which the indépendantistes so love to hate – is in their interests or not. Perhaps it is of supreme indifference to them. But they must be prepared for the next step – for negotiating with and taking on the United States single-handedly as a small nation of six million with a language and culture for which the Americans could not give a good god damn. There will be no France and no *francophonie* to bail them out. They will have to look to their own resources, their own financial reserves, their own collective will.

Perhaps they will find that will. But I hazard a guess that there will be no small number of Québécois – including the very entrepreneurs, the *nouveaux guerriers*, we have been hearing so much about – who will be the first to decry any drop in profit margins or standard of living necessitated by measures to protect the Quebec economy or culture. They will not be prepared to push restrictive language legislation to the hilt if the *Americans* start to complain and threaten Quebec's trading relations with them. These Québécois may find the cost of Quebec's social services too high. They may think too much is being made of cultural nationalism in the new Quebec, at the expense of really important economic issues.

Does this read too much like a scare scenario? Perhaps. Once the hard debate begins, however – that is to say, once English Canada makes it clear that it means business no less than Quebec – some of the scales just may begin to fall from people's eyes. And the sacred union between Bourassa-style continentalists and Parizeau-style continentalists that has held sway over Quebec public opinion in recent years may begin to fall apart. Let me cite two lucid commentaries by Québécois writers who may see a little further in these matters than the political chorus line from the *Folies Bergères* that has had Quebec in its grip.

Marcel Rioux, one of the wisest sociologists of his generation (with impeccable nationalist credentials to boot), writes as follows:

The historical enemy for the Québécois has been "les anglais" of Montreal and Canada, who were perceived as the closest transmission belts for the imperialism of the British or American conquerors. Today, when the Americans have long since displaced the British and are in the process through treaties of carrying through their domination of Quebec and of Canada, the Québécois persist in refusing to see what is happening. An old Chinese proverb sums up our situation: it is difficult to find a black cat in a dark room, but it is even more difficult to find it if you don't bother looking. We will persist in trying to find all that is horrible about the "maudits anglais" of Montreal. The idea of joining with them and other Canadians to limit the damage of continentalism is today interpreted as sabotage, if not treason. It is as though Upper Canada remains the enemy.*

* Marcel Rioux, *Un peuple dans le siècle* (Montréal: Boréal 1990), 254 (my translation).

And Jules-Pascal Venne, a younger political scientist, observes:

Too many indépendantistes have lost sight of the realities that have a crucial impact for the very existence of the Quebec nation or community. Independence will change nothing about Quebec's geopolitical situation, namely the presence next door of the most powerful country in the world. We forget too easily that American society is characterized by a capacity for cultural assimilation that has rarely been equalled by any country in history. We are not paying enough attention to the enormous pressures that will be placed on our health and social security programs within the framework of free trade. There will be similar pressures applied to the whole structure of relations between private Quebec companies and state corporations, so crucial to the emergence of our new capitalist class. These are hard geopolitical factors that no rhetoric will alter. It is in Quebec's interest to maintain privileged relations with Canada in order to counterbalance American pressures.*

Let intellectuals and students, trade unionists and feminists, even some of Quebec's editorial writers, ponder these arguments. Let them begin to ask themselves some hard questions about the United States, questions that Lucien Bouchard and Jacques Parizeau and Gil Rémillard do not seem to ask themselves. The people of Quebec will have to reach their own conclusions. But if, in the ripeness of time, they decide that they may need English Canada at least as much as English Canada may need Quebec if we are both to survive, they will find interlocutors in English Canada – interlocutors, I would add, who are not wedded to the existing federal arrangements and who are perfectly prepared to move on to something different between our two nations; interlocutors who have no illusions about the geopolitical implications of living next door to the

---

*Jules-Pascal Venne, "La question nationale entre deux décennies," *Possibles* 14, no. 2 (Spring 1990): 155–6 (my translation).

most powerful nation on earth; interlocutors who will have the good grace not to gloatingly tell their Québécois friends, "We told you so."

7

Toward an Institutional Restructuring

The American colossus may well provide the overriding imperative for maintaining a Canada-Quebec ensemble in the northern half of North America. The discussion that has preceded, however, also points to the need for a major institutional restructuring in this country. There is the need for a quite different relationship between English Canada and Quebec, one based on the reality of two sociological nations. And there is the need, even before we can work out the modalities of any such restructuring, for a quite new set of political institutions for English Canada. Let us approach these in reverse order, recognizing that if English Canada cannot get its own act together first, we will be in no position to negotiate any new arrangements with Quebec.

Earlier, I sought to define English Canada as the nine provinces and two territories of Canada without Quebec. I suggested that language was a unifying thread for a large majority of its inhabitants and that a shared history and culture, albeit linked to the larger Canadian experience, also played an integral part. The population of English Canada is geographically dispersed among five major regions – the Maritimes, Ontario, the Prairies, British Columbia, and the North – each with its own particular relationship with the country (in the case of Newfoundland, a relationship somewhat different from that of other provinces). It is also important to underline the ethnic diversity of English-speaking Canada when we examine the origins of its people, and the vital importance of aboriginal people to its fabric.

My assumption, and I think it is a correct one, is that English Canadians, regardless of region, wish to continue to live as members of a single nation or nation-state. There is little evidence that British Columbians or Manitobans or Prince Edward Islanders are eager to go it alone, if one means by this sovereign provinces no longer bound up with the rest of the country. There is somewhat more evidence of support for the notion of a sovereign West as an alternative to an English Canadian state. This is seemingly a more serious challenge, since, in strictly economic terms, a sovereign West, with a population of seven and a half million, a territory twice the size of either Quebec or Ontario, and ample resources, seems no less viable a proposition than a sovereign Quebec or a sovereign Ontario. (The Maritimes would have greater problems making a go of it, as would the two territories, with a combined population of under 100,000.) There is, moreover, a history of western alienation and resentment of Central Canada's stranglehold over federal institutions that might be channelled into such a cause.

Yet I think we misread the signals. Many in the West have felt, not entirely incorrectly, that, despite a steadily growing population, their voices have been drowned out in a federal system where Quebec and Ontario together have accounted for three-fifths to two-thirds of the seats in the House of Commons. They have seen the major political parties form governments in which representation from these two key provinces was top-heavy. Provinces like Alberta have often found themselves voting for members of Parliament consigned en bloc to the opposition benches. The national agenda, especially since the 1960s, has been tilted – many in the West would say overwhelmingly – in favour of Quebec, with the Meech Lake constitutional round the final straw. Western concerns (e.g., Senate reform) have in comparison had great difficulty gaining a hearing at the federal level.

The West, in its own way, feels as profoundly Canadian as Ontario or the Maritimes. It is significant, to my mind, that Manitoba's all-party constitutional committee, following public hearings, came up with the call for a Canada clause as a preamble to the constitution, one that would emphasize the fundamental equality of all Canadians as well as the diversity of people who make up the country. This was not the call for a Western Canada or a Manitoba clause, quite the contrary. I think it equally significant that the Reform Party, with a strong base of support in Alberta and some spillover influence in Saskatchewan and British Columbia, is not calling for Canada's dismantling or for an independent West; its slogan is "The West Wants In," and it is pushing for institutional arrangements that would give the West greater influence at the *national* level. Here in British Columbia, Ottawa-bashing may well be a practice indulged in by successive premiers; there is little carry-over of all this to federal voting behaviour, and only the slimmest likelihood that a regionalist party with sovereignty as its objective would make a breakthrough at that level.

All this, however, is not to deny that regional crosscurrents and divisions within English Canada will have to be addressed in any political restructuring. If one starts with the simple observation that Ontario by itself makes up about 50 percent of the population of English Canada, if one makes the analogy with the role that Prussia played in Imperial Germany after 1871, then one might fear that Ontario, acting as a bloc, could indeed overwhelm the rest. It would seem we need to find a way to balance off its weight and ensure that a government for English Canada was not simply a government for Ontario.

This is not the same thing as advocating a government against Ontario; one does not correct for one possible inequity by introducing a second. Ontario, geographically, remains at the centre of English Canada, economically and politically as well. We will get nowhere, if we are to pull English Canada together, by indulging in Ontario-bashing, any more than in the bashing of other provinces. What we simply need to do is to balance off Ontario's strength and legitimate claims to a role in national affairs with those of the outlying regions and provinces.

The way we can do this with minimal headaches is by going the route of an elected Senate. On the assumption that we retain a parliamentary system for English Canada, representation in the House of Commons, once Quebec stops sending members, would continue to be based on population. Ontario, under the present circumstances, would have close to 50 percent of the members, the western provinces somewhere around 35 percent, the Atlantic provinces and the territories the remainder.

But the Senate, with Quebec removed, would be a different proposition. Ontario's twenty-four senators would make up less than a third of the remaining seventy-eight, although we might well want to make some adjustments in the numbers allowed the different provinces (and the territories, which are presently excluded). Such adjustments would seem all the more necessary since the Senate we are talking about would almost surely be elected in order to genuinely represent the *vox populi* in the different regions. An appointed Senate filled with political cronies is simply not up to the task.

The advocates of a triple-E Senate (elected, effective, and equal) might argue for the absolute equality of each province (and perhaps territory) in a new upper house. There is the American, as well as Australian, precedent, in which the states have equal representation in such a chamber. I cannot help wondering, however, with what justice one would allow Prince Edward Island with 120,000 people or Newfoundland with 600,000 equal representation with Ontario's 10 million. A plausible argument can be made for a system that gives smaller provinces greater representation than the large ones, but not on a scale of 100 to 1 or 20 to 1. Moreover, if we want our Senate to be effective and play a role in national affairs perhaps even greater than the House of Commons in certain respects, it will have to be seen as a legitimate forum by every region, large no less than small. Equal representation would thwart this purpose and be seen as short-changing Ontario in particular.

A sliding scale makes more sense. Ontario, for example, might keep its twenty-four senators; in the West, provinces like British Columbia or Alberta might be given twelve senators each, Manitoba and Saskatchewan six each; six each might also be allocated to Nova Scotia, New Brunswick, and Newfoundland, with PEI getting two and each of the territories one. (The provision going back to 1867 for a certain minimum number of House of Commons seats for the different Atlantic provinces could be retained.) This would make for a total of eighty-two divided up as follows: the West, thirty-six; Ontario, twenty-four; the Atlantic provinces, twenty; and the North, two. Ontario would have about 30 percent of the senators under this scheme as compared to almost 50 percent of the Commons seats; yet its contingent would be the single largest, twice as large as that from each of the next two provinces, British Columbia or Alberta; and its representation would be greater than that of the Atlantic provinces combined, with about 2 million people. Conversely, the western provinces would make up the largest single bloc; together with the Atlantic provinces and the North, their 70 percent of Senate seats would more than outweigh Ontario's representation.

The point of this exercise is not to advance figures or ratios written in stone. There is room for continuing debate about the principles underlying, or regarding, the exact contingent to be given each province if we want to take population into some account. I could certainly live with a different set of figures, and so, I think, could most Canadians. The principles that must underline Senate reform, however, are fairly straightforward: (1) the peripheral regions must be given greater voice, and (2) Ontario should not find itself completely overwhelmed. The triple-E proposal fails, in my eyes, because it does not respect the second principle.

For all the inevitable haggling over the exact composition of an elected Senate, in the end, it should be crystal clear that there is no surer way than this of addressing the feeling of regional grievance that might otherwise tear English Canada apart. I would add that the experience of other federal systems with elected upper houses suggests that these help channel regional sentiments into political authority at the national level; to that degree, upper houses help counteract the role of governors or premiers as the sole guardians of their bailiwicks. The Achilles heel of Canadian federalism in recent decades has been the growing power of provincial premiers over national affairs. It began with a series of federal-provincial constitutional conferences in the 1960s and 1970s; it became a festering problem with their ever-greater frequency after the constitutional patriation of 1982. Meech Lake, had it gone through, would have made these a permanent fixture of our political lives and rendered it impossible to introduce some real accountability, to the citizens at large, on the part of provincial premiers with respect to constitutional matters.

Electing senators – whether we do this on a proportional representation basis within each province, which seems the fairest, or on some territorial basis within each province, which risks duplicating House of Commons allocations – gives people a direct say on how regional interests will be articulated at the national level. It simultaneously introduces some limits, through both the party system and the nationalizing influence of a second chamber, on just how far these regional sentiments will be taken. It is all very well for grievances to be voiced, as frequently and loudly as necessary, within an elected upper house, and for an English Canadian government worth its salt to take them into account, but at the same time, there is a national government to be run, which implies something more than the sum of regional concerns. Senators elected to a national parliament are much more likely to have a national focus than premiers whose mandate extends no further than provincial borders.

What I have not discussed so far are the exact powers we might want to give our elected Senate and the other changes that might be expected in the operation of a federal government now confined to English Canada. The British system of government, under which we have been operating since 1867, rests on the greatest power lying in the House of Commons. Once we move from an appointed to an elected Senate, we would clearly expect the Senate to have some real authority. Its members will, after all, have no less of a popular mandate than members of the Commons. Yet something of the old distribution of power between the two houses should be retained, with the Commons, for most matters, the more important of the two. There must also be a way of dealing with the conflicts that may arise (as they have in Australia) when one political party has a majority in the lower house, but only a minority in the upper. The most sensible proposal to my mind was contained in the Macdonald Commission report,* calling for a six-month suspensive veto by the Senate over House of Commons legislation. This means that the Senate could hold up the passage of government legislation for up to six months, but no longer; legislation would automatically come into effect thereafter, assuming it had passed the House of Commons a second time.

Supporters of a strong Senate – and of the regional principle it represents – might find this altogether too cavalier. Why bother going through all the trouble of electing a Senate if, in the end, it has only a limited power of delay? Could not Ontario continue to hog it over English Canada by ensuring a government favourable to it controlled the House of Commons? The answer to this might run as follows: (1) The power of delay, in some instances, is itself an important check, especially against hastily conceived or poorly drafted legislation. It gives time, moreover, for a more extensive public debate to take place. (2) Governments would be made up of members primarily from the Commons but also from the Senate. In trying to keep English Canada

---

* *Report of the Royal Commission on the Economic Union and Development Prospects for Canada*, vol. 3 (Ottawa, 1985), 86–92.

together, they would have to be especially sensitive to its regional dimensions, something the Senate, in particular, would ensure. (3) On all constitutional matters, the powers of the Senate would equal those of the Commons. (I leave for consideration shortly a possible Senate role in a Canada-Quebec Union, one that could be very important indeed.)

There would be other changes in the operation of a national government for English Canada. It is very unlikely that bilingualism or the Official Languages Act could survive once Quebec decided, for most purposes, to go its own way. English would become the only official language for Parliament, the federal civil service, and most courts; the relevant language provisions in the Charter of Rights would have to be rewritten. New Brunswick, with its large Acadian population, might well retain official bilingualism, and we could certainly make provision for some French-language services elsewhere in Canada where the numbers warrant. Reciprocal provisions for minority-language rights might even be negotiated between the English Canadian provinces (or English Canada as a whole) and Quebec. But the entrenched position of French at the federal level and a status formally equal to English would become a thing of the past.

The Supreme Court would lose its three Quebec justices and have to be reconstituted as a court with six, seven, or nine justices for English Canada alone. Federal departments, from Labour to National Health and Welfare or Justice, would have similarly redefined mandates. And all our constitutional documents would have to be rewritten to apply to English Canada alone. This, by itself, would require an exercise in constitution-making as extensive as, and hopefully a good deal more democratic than, any we have known until now.

We might also want to tackle the distribution of powers between centre and provinces. Should we keep these exactly as before, should there be some shift in powers, or should there be greater co-ordination of activities between the two levels than previously? For example, higher education is an area where the federal government currently provides about 50 percent of all government funding as well as the lion's share of support for research in medicine, the sciences, engineering, the social sciences, and the humanities. Would it not be logical to create a ministry of higher education for English Canada to work along with the provinces in this field, or, to go one step further, to consider shifting the responsibility for higher education entirely to the federal government, in exchange, perhaps, for giving the provinces complete control over day care? With Quebec removed for most purposes, we need no longer have any inhibitions in advocating a greater national role for Ottawa in areas like higher education.

All this may sound very tantalizing, even if we postpone the ticklish question of how we might get to such a stage. What about Quebec in all this? In what areas exactly will we maintain common structures and how might these decisions be implemented? There will be no Quebec members of Parliament or of the Senate serving in the Parliament of English Canada, no Quebec ministers in its cabinet. Nor will English Canada send representatives to Quebec's National Assembly. Does each government simply name delegates to certain joint bodies that are, in turn, responsible for running the economic and any other activities that we agree to share?

This is what the Parti Québécois's proposals for sovereignty-association would have amounted to. They are, however, totally inadequate to the task at hand, which goes well beyond economic matters and, in any case, presupposed two sovereign states – English Canada and Quebec – negotiating with one another as equals. Neither English Canada nor Quebec would be fully sovereign in the type of confederal arrangements I am about to propose. And the members of both societies, through elected representatives and appropriate constitutional procedures, would have a real say in what took place at the confederal level, without the direct intercession of the governments of English Canada or Quebec.

This may sound rather confusing. Am I proposing a third elected tier of government for English Canada, beyond the provinces and the newly constituted government of English Canada? Will Quebec have a two-tiered system, one rooted in the National Assembly and the other in this new confederal relationship with English Canada? How would one expect such a contraption to fly? And would English Canadians, in particular, already saddled with two levels of government, take kindly to the notion of yet a third?

What I would advocate is neither as cumbersome as three completely different levels of governments for English Canada, nor is it a system in which confederal institutions are but the creature of the governments of English Canada and of Quebec. It would, indeed, be asking too much of English Canadians to expect them to elect members to a Parliament of the Canada-Quebec Union, on top of the provincial and federal members and now senators that they will be choosing. Why not, instead, give the Senate a further – and very important – function? Why not let its members, who will now be able to speak with some real authority for the provinces that have elected them, represent us collectively in the future Parliament of the Canada-Quebec Unions? The people of Quebec, for their part, could directly elect a number of representatives to join them, equal to Quebec's share of the population of Canada as a whole. Thus, if Quebec has 24–25 percent of our total population, it could elect twenty-seven members to sit alongside the eighty-two senators from English Canada in the Parliament of the Union.

On the English Canadian side, therefore, the Senate acquires a double function – as the elected upper house of the Parliament of English Canada and as the elected English Canadian component of the Parliament of the Canada–Quebec Union. It will be for Québécois to decide whether to give their twenty-seven elected representatives in the Parliament of the Union any additional responsibilities vis-à-vis the National Assembly.

A key function of the Union Parliament will be to approve the ministers who will constitute the governments of the Union.

The governmental functions vested in the Union would include foreign policy, defence, international trade, finance (including currency), environmental matters, and citizenship. There might be others – were English Canada and Quebec to so decide – but these functions will constitute the core. They touch on the key attributes of sovereignty and on Canada's role as an actor in international affairs. They maintain a common citizenship between the people of our two nations. They encompass responsibility for the Bank of Canada, for our participation in international organizations like the International Monetary Fund (IMF) or the World Bank, and – with appropriate powers of taxation to back this up – for the national debt. They include the new and complex area of the environment, which transcends traditional territorial boundaries. Ministers could be members of the Parliament of Canada or of the Quebec National Assembly/ Quebec parliamentary delegation to the Union. The head of government or prime minister of the Union would normally be the prime minister or head of government of English Canada or of Quebec.

There would be a certain rotation between English Canadians and Québécois when it came to the ministries of the Union, though inevitably English Canadians would outnumber their Quebec counterparts in a ratio, let us say, of at least 2 to 1. Bilingualism would be retained in the Parliament of the Union and all confederal ministries. On taking office, a government of the Union would have to win a vote of confidence from the Parliament of the Union. Laws would need parliamentary approval, there would be parliamentary committees with appropriate powers, and so on. The government of the Union would be responsible for crown corporations that English Canada and Quebec wished to keep intact and for the administration of projects like the St Lawrence Seaway.

There would be a head of state with powers equivalent to those of a governor general, whether we keep that name or opt for a president instead. The head would be designated for a five-year term by a joint meeting of the Parliament of English Canada and the Quebec National Assembly/Quebec parliamentary delegation to the Union. Here the principle of rotation could be scrupulously observed. Depending on whether he or she came from English Canada or Quebec, the head of state could also serve as head of state for that government; there could be an associate head of state who could serve as head of state for the other government.

I could go on. But I am in danger of indulging in the favourite pastime of jurists and constitutional lawyers and producing a laundry list of functions and powers that may or may not meet with approval. Let me instead focus on two or three questions of principle, leaving the fine points for future discussion.

A key element in my proposal, then, is a third level of government for English Canada and a second for Quebec, feeding, however, on existing structures. An elected English Canadian Senate will be there in any case and needn't be invented just for purposes of the Union. There will be prime ministers for English Canada and Quebec; we do not have to designate a new one for the Union. Ministers can be seconded from the two national legislatures, and key ministries such as External Affairs, Defence, Finance, or Trade already exist, as does the Bank of Canada; nothing needs to be done to set these in motion.

There could be problems, I suppose, if the party composition in the Parliament of the Union were significantly different from the one in either the Canadian House of Commons or the Quebec National Assembly; it is theoretically possible for the senators from English Canada and the elected Quebec representatives to the Union Parliament to have other party allegiances. This would require some of the same political skill the Americans deploy when they have an administration of one party and a congressional majority of the other; or the French, faced with a National Assembly and president of opposite colours.

More serious might be the concern of a province such as Ontario, that it might be short-changed when it comes to representation in the Parliament of the Union. It is one thing to accept a greater role for the smaller provinces in the upper house of a parliament in which the lower house is based on representation by population. But now that the Senate becomes a key parliamentary body in matters of foreign policy, defence, or external trade, is it right to give less populous provinces greater weight? This is a delicate question and it may require some further adjustment in the proportionate strength of the different regions within the Senate of English Canada. Should Ontario be given representation at least equal to that of the West as a whole, or at the very least, equal to the number of representatives that Quebec would be sending to the Parliament of the Union? Too top-heavy a regional tilt in a Senate that also serves as part of the Parliament for the Union could engender strong grievances in Ontario.

Further, there will have to be some kind of written document, to be agreed to by both English Canada and Quebec, to regulate the affairs of the Union. Such a document would be in addition to the constitutions English Canada and Quebec would have to frame to regulate their internal affairs. There would presumably also have to be some kind of constitutional court, perhaps made up of judges from our two supreme courts, to adjudicate any problems of interpretation or jurisdiction that might arise.

So things do become more complicated when we start thinking in terms of two sociological nations rather than one. But is there any alternative, other than a federalism that most Québécois no longer want and a sovereignty-association arrangement that English Canadians would reject out of hand? I think not. Does the will exist to introduce a scheme of this sort? That remains to be seen. And can we actually find a means for bringing both a government of English Canada and a Canada-Quebec Union into being?

8

Constituent Assemblies for
English Canada and Quebec

There are a number of ways a people can go about framing a constitution. It can be introduced over their heads by their leaders in the aftermath of a successful war, as with the 1871 constitution of Imperial Germany, or in a conscious attempt to emulate such a model, as with the Japanese constitution of 1889; both kept the elective, democratic element in a lower house while giving powers to check and balance it to an aristocratic upper house and vesting enormous powers in the kaiser/emperor. A constitution may be written in the aftermath of successful revolution or liberation from an occupying or imperial power. The Americans went through such an experience in 1787, the French on more than one occasion from 1789 on, the Latin American countries in the nineteenth century, and most of the countries of Asia and Africa in our own. The American constitution was subject to popular ratification of a sort in the thirteen states and is still in effect after two centuries; France has had as many constitutions as it has had regime changes since its revolution, though its current constitution, ratified by referendum in October 1958 in the aftermath of de Gaulle's return to power and with a strong presidency to balance the National Assembly, looks as though it may endure. Latin America, too often, has known constitutions more honoured in the breach than the observance, although the current phase of transition from authoritarianism bodes somewhat better for liberal democracy in that continent than the recent past. The Indian constitution, drafted by a constituent assembly in 1946, has endured rather better than observers might have predicted. In too many of the other post-colonial societies of Africa and Asia, constitutionalism, since independence, has proven the exception.

In Canada, we have not known constitution-making as the authoritarian practice that took place in nineteenth-century Germany or Japan, but neither have we known the more democratic style of constitution-making pioneered by the United States and France. The BNA Act was the product of several behind-closed-doors conferences, most notably at Charlottetown and Quebec, grouping key colonial politicians of the day; there was limited public discussion of what transpired, nor was the text of the BNA Act submitted for ratification to the assemblies of the federating colonies – Nova Scotia, New Brunswick, the United Canadas – let alone to the population as such. The measure, as John A. Macdonald boasted in a letter to Leonard Tilley, had to be carried *per saltum*, with maximum speed and minimum public deliberation. He was to get his way with a document quickly steered through the British Parliament, reflecting in form and content a less than democratic set of values.

True, the BNA Act was modelled on the constitution of Great Britain and provided for a parliamentary form of government. And by the latter part of the nineteenth century, effective power lay neither with the House of Lords nor the monarchy, but with the House of Commons. The forms of the British constitution, however, reflected a feudal and early modern past in which king/queen and lords were more than ornaments in affairs of state; there was, accordingly, a strong bias in the institutional structures of Great Britain against too direct or vocal a role for the lower orders – that is, the people – in political affairs. The bias lay in favour of sovereignty vested in King/Queen-in-Parliament, with a civil service and military in which those of either aristocratic or gentrified background commanded, and a judiciary sage and respectful of property, status, and order.

These elements of British political culture were part of the political package that we took over when the Fathers of Confederation made the British constitution their guiding light. There is not a single reference in the text of the BNA Act to the people, to democracy, or to what might be called popular sovereignty. There is a good deal about the Crown, about the Senate, about the Commons, about the division of power between federal and provincial governments, but the people as such do not figure at all. Not only were they not the political subject of our constitution, they had no direct role to play in either helping to frame or to ratify it. This is the way Canada's nineteenth-century political leaders conceived of constitutions and constitution-making when they set about creating a new country.

For over a hundred years thereafter, nothing was to change in this regard. Constitutional amendments would, from time to time, be forwarded to Westminster, sometimes through the initiative of the federal Parliament alone, more often following consultation with and the approval of the provinces. Although Manitoba might experiment with the direct initiative or repeal in the 1910s and Alberta with notions of delegate democracy in the 1920s and 1930s, there was little possibility for such experimentation to spread beyond their borders. The temper of establishment opinion in Canada, especially at the federal level, was strongly opposed to direct popular input into national affairs, favouring instead the people's indirect role of choosing from competing candidates and political parties in periodic elections. Expanding this role through provision for referendum approval of key pieces of government legislation, let alone constitutional changes, would be interpreted as un-British, un-Canadian, and *lèse-majesté* of *lèse-majestés*, anti-parliamentary.

Fortunately, we have begun to mature as a people and pay some attention to what has been occurring in other countries and under other climes. We have ceased to take parliamentary norms and forms as the last word in democratic theory in a period when, even in Britain, groups like Charter 88 are calling for a written charter of rights to protect the liberties of British citizens against encroachment by their own government. Some of our own social movements, from feminists to environmentalists, have learned to spurn an all-too-Canadian deference to authority. Canadians today have much less reason to trust their elected governments to carry through with wholesale constitutional change; instead, they would prefer that key initiatives be submitted for some form of popular approval. The Burkean notion of members of parliament (or legislatures) owing their electors nothing but their consciences carries less weight, as does the derived notion of first ministers with parliamentary majorities being free to act pretty well as they wish, even in constitutional matters. Decidedly Rousseauean, and Jeffersonian notions of popular sovereignty have suddenly begun to take hold.

The transformation was helped along, in my opinion, by Quebec's adopting the referendum approach to determining its own constitutional status back in the late 1970s. The Parti Québécois – here more French or American in outlook than British – accepted the overriding character of the sovereignty-association option and was prepared to submit it, in modified form, to the electorate as a whole. There were tactical reasons, to be sure, for the PQ's deferring its constitutional option to a future referendum. Twice, in 1970 and 1973, it had lost its bid for office by failing to separate its constitutional option from its program of government. Further, the logic of a referendum took a powerful hold in Quebec in the years and months preceding 20 May 1980, and the device came to be seen as the legitimate way for resolving such crucial matters, both by proponents and opponents of sovereignty-association. To that degree, events in Quebec may well have opened the door to demands for greater input into constitutional matters in the rest of Canada.

Something of this would surface in the 1980–81 debate over patriation of the Canadian constitution and the Charter of Rights. The principal actors in this debate were, as usual, first ministers, ministers of justice or intergovernmental affairs, and high-ranking civil servants or advisers. Proposals were drafted within these circles, and the final package, for the most part, was worked out through closely guarded negotiations behind closed doors. This time, however, there was a greater mobilization of opinion than had been true in 1864–67, and some popular input into the process. A special joint parliamentary committee heard hundreds of briefs, many carefully argued, and incorporated some of the changes proposed into the Charter; women's groups and aboriginal peoples were able to secure further changes through mass public meetings and demonstrations, even after the constitutional package had been approved on 5 November 1981; and at least two key actors in the whole debate, Trudeau and Lévesque – significantly, both from Quebec – were prepared, in one brief moment of agreement, to suggest submitting the entire package for popular approval through referendum. This was resisted at the time by the English Canadian premiers, wedded to notions of parliamentary and legislative, as opposed to popular, supremacy.

The content of the Charter of Rights and Freedoms may have had a lot to do with the degree of popular interest that the 1980–81 constitutional negotiations sparked. It is fair to say that there was a good deal less interest manifested in the spring of 1987, when Meech Lake was initially sprung upon the country. The notion that the constitution was something that belonged to the people of Canada, not merely to the politicians, had, however, been planted in the early 1980s and would grow with the unfolding pattern of Charter adjudication over the decade. It would prove difficult over time to scupper demands for broad popular consultation on a constitutional package that was not without its effects vis-à-vis federal power and, through the distinct society clause, Charter rights as well. The inner circle of first ministers and their advisers significantly underestimated this factor in their calculations of June 1987.

The rest is history. What we need to do now is draw the lessons from the failure of the Meech process and from our earlier, less-than-democratic tradition of constitution-making. We need to do so because the agenda before us, if what I have been arguing in this essay is correct, is a good deal more charged than the one of 1987 or even that of 1980–81. We need to develop a set of political arrangements for the governance of English Canada. We may need to rethink the division of powers between centre and provinces and some of the provisions of the Charter, on language rights, for example. We need to address the question of an elected Senate. We need to tackle the question of aboriginal rights in a satisfactory and, hopefully, lasting fashion. And, last but not least, we need to work out a looser, confederal arrangement with Quebec.

How do we go about this? By leaving it to a federal government headed by Brian Mulroney or Jean Chrétien – each from Quebec – to do it for us, in conjunction with premiers who may, or may not, have some particular qualification to represent their provincial electorate in matters constitutional? Clearly something would be wanting from such a process, even if, for cosmetic reasons, our *nomenklatura* of elected prime minister and premiers were prepared to allow for some consultative process through parliamentary and legislative committees before the final text of any agreement had been sealed in wax. We have surely learned from recent events to be less trusting. We are faced, moreover, with a complex and challenging rearrangement of the very nature of Canada that is certain to elicit a good deal of popular concern. And so it should.

There is only one way we can hope to tackle such an agenda and win the stamp of democratic approval in the process – by going the route of a democratically elected constituent assembly. This is a route that other countries have travelled in periods of crisis or change. It is one I wish we had travelled back in the 1860s, when John A. Macdonald and his cohorts favoured a more elitist style of constitution-making in its place, or in 1980–81, when Pierre Trudeau set about to patriate the constitution. It is one we may have no choice but to travel in the 1990s, as the federal arrangements that have bound English Canada to Quebec until now fall apart.

How would such an assembly come to be chosen? What would its mandate be? How can we synchronize what English Canadians may desire by way of confederal arrangements and what Québécois may want? And how, in the end, could we be sure that anything such a body decided was indeed acceptable to the citizens of Canada as a whole?

It is my firm belief that we need a constituent assembly for English Canada distinct from any constituent assembly that Quebec itself might elect. We need, in other words, an assembly with representatives from the nine provinces and two territories to address the question of institutional arrangements within English Canada and the constitutional provisions by which we will be bound. If what we are doing is giving political expression to a sociological nation named English Canada, Quebec as such has no direct role to play. That would be as anachronistic as to expect English Canadian representatives to take part in the deliberations of a Quebec constituent assembly.

An English Canadian constituent assembly might be convened as the result of a joint decision of the Parliament of Canada and, say, a two-thirds majority of the English Canadian provinces. Its members would be elected in proportions closely reflecting the respective populations of the different provinces and territories and their representation in the House of Commons. Ideally, these elections would take place on a proportional representation basis within each province or within heavily populated subdivisions of the larger provinces (e.g., Metro Toronto, BC's Lower Mainland). Thus, a candidate receiving 20 percent of the vote in a province or provincial subdivision with five seats, or whose name was first on a party list receiving 20 percent, would be elected. Anyone would be free to run, but if that person were a member either of Parliament or a provincial legislature, he or she would have to step down first; membership in both the constituent assembly and some other legislative body would be incompatible.

The constituent assembly should represent a reasonable cross-section of views in Canadian society and, at the same time, be capable of efficacious debate and decision making; I suspect this boils down to a membership somewhere between 100 and 125. To this number should be added a small number of representatives elected directly by the first peoples from across English Canada; four to five representatives may be a little more than their actual share of the total population would suggest, but salient enough to have some impact.

In any election to such an assembly, we can be sure that a range of options would be presented to the citizenry. Some candidates would have a strong federalist orientation, meaning they would favour a strong central government for English Canada; others, just as strongly, might favour greater power for the provinces. Conservatives and others on the right might make much about the need to entrench property rights in any revised charter; social democrats and left liberals would argue just as strongly for the entrenchment of social rights (e.g., medical insurance, education, the right of workers to organize collectively). Some candidates would present themselves as proponents of confederal arrangements with Quebec; others would seek to hold on to as much of existing federal structures as possible; still others might argue for a complete severance of ties between English Canada and Quebec. The cards would not be stacked in favour of any particular option; candidates with a high profile in their own province and/or with effective party backing would find themselves sitting in the constituent assembly.

The assembly would establish its own procedures and be free to commission reports and engage in public hearings as it saw fit. Its deliberations would be open and, one suspects, surrounded with a fair degree of drama; philosophical principles would be debated, along with the nitty-gritty of specific proposals. Quite clearly, the assembly would be charting the constitutional course for a nation and, in areas like Senate reform, opening up new terrain.

With representation by population the assembly's own underlying principle, it might seem to be stacked against a Senate giving greater power to the smaller provinces. I tend to think this unlikely for the simple reason that the impetus behind the entire enterprise is the need to come up with arrangements that will keep English Canada together. This means satisfying the perfectly legitimate demands of the outlying regions for some means of balancing off the power of the single, strongest province – Ontario. Trade-offs will probably also take place between proponents of a strong centre and those favouring strong provinces, between advocates of left-of-centre Charter provisions and those hewing to a more conservative position. To that degree, the assembly would be an accurate microcosm of the larger (English) Canadian ensemble.

The aboriginal representatives could be expected to voice native people's concern for the entrenchment of native rights in the new English Canadian constitutional order. There is no guarantee that they would get all that they want, but they would certainly get a thorough hearing and, in all likelihood, acknowledgment in a final document of the place of Canada's first peoples and perhaps some constitutionally recognized form of self-government.

No electoral provision, I think, could guarantee a specific percentage of representatives in the assembly for women, who make up 50 percent of the total population, ethnic groups, or the francophone minority. However, in the normal course of events, one would expect candidates to the assembly, especially those put forward by the different political parties, to represent a fair cross-section of English Canadian society in terms of gender, ethnic origin, or linguistic minorities.

It would make sense to set a specific time limit for the deliberations of a constituent assembly. Twelve months? Eighteen? Twenty-four? It is hard to say, but we certainly do not want an assembly dragging its work out for years. The single most important check on its activities would be the provision that any package it finally agrees to will have to be presented to the electorate at large for ratification in a referendum. A new constitution, in order to come into effect, would require majority approval across English Canada, with support in at least six of the nine provinces. Such a constitutional package would presumably be presented for acceptance or rejection en bloc. It would be too cumbersome to proceed otherwise, and unrealistic to expect the electorate to pronounce on each and every clause.

So far, arrangements with Quebec have been left out. These too would fall within the purview of the assembly, as they would within that of any constitutent assembly Quebec chose to elect. Quebec's assembly, like English Canada's, would have to be representative of that society's diversity. Right, centre, and left would jockey for position; some might argue for a presidential type regime, others a parliamentary; some would advocate close relations with English Canada, others little or none. Aboriginal peoples and the province's anglophone minority would presumably have a place in the deliberations, alongside the francophone majority. Much of this assembly's time, at least initially, would be taken up with framing a constitution for Quebec, but no small part of its subsequent activities would be directed to working out arrangements with English Canada. And the reverse would be true as well.

Ideally, each of the two constituent assemblies would deliberate separately and come up with its own set of proposals. At some point, however, or perhaps on more than one occasion, it would make sense to have the two assemblies meet together and exchange views. It will probably also prove necessary to strike a committee from each assembly to negotiate with the other to try to work out an acceptable common framework.

On the assumption that a majority in each assembly in the end favours some sort of a Canada-Quebec Union (or whatever other name one chooses to give it), there will have to be a written text spelling out its exact powers and mode of operation. Provision will also have to be made for settling disputes regarding jurisdiction or substance that may arise, and for future amendments to the document.

Let me be optimistic and suggest that at the end of the day – twelve or eighteen months after the process has been initiated – agreement between the English Canadian and Quebec constituent assemblies will have been reached. Let me further assume that by then the constitutional arrangements governing each of the two entities, English Canada and Quebec, will be complete. It should at that time be possible to submit not only a constitution to the electorate of English Canada (and ditto for Quebec), but also the basic document of the Canada-Quebec Union as well. The document establishing the Union would come into effect if it received 50 percent or more approval in both English Canada and Quebec. (English Canada might also want it to pass the test of approval in at least six of the nine provinces.) If it failed in either, it would go down to defeat.

Some readers may not share my optimism. The acrimony that has coloured English Canada-Quebec relations over the past two years, they might argue, is certain to taint any deliberations between two elected constituent assemblies somewhere down the line. Will not the tendency be for hard-liners on either side – bitter enemies of Quebec and things French on the one, obdurate foes of English Canada and *le fait anglais* on the other – to drown out the advocates of more moderate positions? Won't Quebec ask for too much by way of control over the government of any Canada-Quebec Union, for example? Will English Canadians be comfortable sharing powers over the Bank of Canada or foreign policy or the armed forces with a Quebec defined as a sociological nation and with political structures quite distinct from English Canada's? The sceptics would seem to have a lot going for them.

My deep conviction, however, is that a majority, both in English Canada and in Quebec, want something other than the complete rupture that a sovereign English Canada and a sovereign Quebec would herald. They will not elect majorities with sovereignty as their bottom line to either assembly. They will expect hard bargaining by the constituent assembly they have elected with the assembly of the other; but they will also expect some of the give and take that has historically characterized relations between anglophones and francophones in this country and that may yet serve us in good stead. In other words, they will expect a minimum of flexibility on the part of the representatives they elect and serious efforts toward laying the basis for some permanent and incontestably legitimate arrangement. The mere fact that any such arrangement must win majority approval in both English Canada and Quebec sets certain limits to what either side can expect; it also sets clear limits to the ability of either to hold the other hostage to impossible demands. Much like the Meech Lake Accord, any unbalanced arrangement would simply fall victim to the conflicting interests of the two sociological majorities.

Elected constituent assemblies are the only certain way we have of breaking the existing constitutional deadlock and giving the people – both of English Canada and of Quebec – some real input into constitutional change. In one fell swoop, it allows us to introduce a genuinely democratic touch into our political culture and puts us on a par with nations around the world for whom popular sovereignty is the necessary underpinning of the modern state. It broadens the pool of constitution-makers from the present inner circle of first ministers to one much more representative of public opinion. It allows both English Canada and Quebec to freely work out the set of internal arrangements that most satisfies them and, no less importantly, the set of confederal arrangements by which they may continue to be linked.

How do we get things rolling? How, in particular, do we get the elected politicians in Ottawa and in the provinces, with their current stranglehold over the constitutional process, to accept so radical a departure? Selflessness has never been one of their sterling qualities – why should they suddenly alter their behaviour at this late date?

The answer is quite simple – because the old way isn't producing results. Most of the participants in the Meech process have publicly stated as much, and there are polls showing overwhelming numbers of English Canadians of the same opinion. The process of first ministers' conferences on constitutional affairs has, in any case, broken down, if Robert Bourassa's oft-repeated refusal to attend these in the future is to be taken seriously. From the point of view of the English Canadian premiers, moreover, there is something to be gained from getting the constitutional tar baby off their backs. Why not leave it to an elected constituent assembly to sort out the mess? Some, at least, of those elected to such an assembly will be strong defenders of provincial interests. And the requirement for referendum approval of any eventual arrangement in at least six of the nine provinces will give the premiers further ammunition in countering any unacceptable scheme.

The federal government and Parliament, for their part, much like our political parties torn by the conflicting interests of English Canada and of Quebec, may find real virtue in the constituent assembly proposal. It will allow each of our sociological nations to sort out its affairs; it will, on the English Canadian side, result in a federal government more cohesive and potentially more effective than is possible under current conditions; and, as between English Canada and Quebec, it holds forth the promise of an ongoing union, which is a good deal better than any sovereignty-association option is likely to do. Having exhausted the consociational elitist route, our federal politicians may just be ready to give democratic constitution-making a chance.

Nothing, however, will happen, unless there is potent popular support for such a course. An essay here or there, an article or radio interview or television clip arguing the case is all very well, but one will need evidence that tens of thousands, hundreds of thousands, of Canadians and Québécois favour such a course. Will we need a mass movement from coast to coast before we see such an initiative take off? Will the hearings of the Bélanger-Campeau Commission in Quebec or of the federally appointed Spicer Commission help bring such demands to the fore? Will we have to try tapping in to existing organizations and movements – from trade unions to women's groups to student councils or aboriginal associations – until all press the same demand on our political system? Those of us who believe in the cause of democratic constitution-making, whether we be English Canadians or Québécois, have our work cut out for us in the months and years to come.

9

The Question of Minority Rights

We may indeed be about to redefine Canada on the basis of two sociological nations, granting to the governments of English Canada and Quebec many of the powers presently vested in the government of Canada. There will be separate constitutions and presumably separate charters or bills of rights for each of our two nations, with provisions that are not necessarily identical. We will be bidding the Official Languages Act adieu, accepting the reality of two predominantly unilingual societies, English in the case of the nine provinces and two territories, French in the case of Quebec.

What happens to minorities under these circumstances? There are over 500,000 anglophones in Quebec, and no small number of allophones, who until now have considered themselves no less English-speaking Canadians than the inhabitants of the other provinces. There are about a million people of French-speaking origin outside Quebec, a majority of whom retain an attachment to the French language and culture. The geographical boundaries of English Canada and Quebec do not neatly coincide with the territory anglophones and francophones inhabit.

It is no secret that the most acute conflicts in today's world occur in societies divided along linguistic, ethnic, or religious lines. Lebanon, Sri Lanka, Kosovo, Azerbaijan, and Uzbekhstan are some of the most recent flashpoints, showing just how potent and destructive ethnic hatreds can become. Even in multilingual or multi-ethnic societies where fratricidal conflicts are contained, resentment can spill over into the political arena, provoking intolerance or backlash. One thinks of the Hungarian minority in Rumania, of the Russian minority in the Baltic republics, of immigrant workers in Europe, or of the Chinese minority throughout much of South East Asia. Minorities – whether rich or poor, originating with nations or nationalities that are economically backward or advanced – inevitably feel themselves threatened when surrounded by nationalistic majorities.

We would be foolish to think that our two linguistic minorities, faced with the type of rearrangement discussed thus far, might not feel themselves threatened. There would still be common citizenship between English Canada and Quebec, free movement back and forth, and common structures at the level of the Canada-Quebec Union. But the essential activities of these communities would take place within the rubric of either English Canada or Quebec. And each of these societies might well be experiencing a wave of nationalist ferment in the aftermath of what its population had just been through.

This question of minority rights is what led the Royal Commission on Bilingualism and Biculturalism in the late 1960s to reject territorial unilingualism as a policy. It was a key part of the rationale behind both the Official Languages Act and the language provisions of the Charter. It remains perhaps the strongest possible reason one can advance for wanting to maintain the type of federal arrangements we have developed, rather than embracing a philosophy based upon two nations.

We have already seen just how acrimonious relations between the two linguistic groups can become when minority rights appear to be under attack. Nothing so inflamed opinion in English Canada as the actions of the Bourassa government in introducing Bill 178 in December 1988; what seemed to a majority of Quebec francophones to be a legitimate measure to protect the integrity of Quebec's sign law, even against the letter of the Charter, was seen as flagrant intolerance toward their own language by a majority of anglophones across the country. The actions of municipal councils like that of Sault Ste Marie in refusing the extension of municipal services in French – on grounds of cost – was seen as patent bias against French Canadians by a vast majority of francophones. Add to this Quebec flag trampling in Brockville and Canadian flag burnings in Quebec and one has the ingredients for nationalist explosion.

What then should we expect if it comes to a parting of the ways – however muted or disguised – between our two nations? Against whom will the *passionarias* of English rights like APEC vent their anger, if not the francophone minorities scattered across English Canada? How much willingness will there be to fund minority French-language schools or community centres in an English Canada forced, somewhat against its will, to define itself as an English-speaking nation side by side with a French-speaking Quebec? Will it be easy for French Canadians to assume their identity in Alberta, Manitoba, or Ontario? Will the English majority in New Brunswick and the Acadian minority win international human rights awards for intercommunal harmony? For their part, will Quebec anglophones (or allophones) easily escape the wrath of Quebec nationalists who pressed to hard to override the Supreme Court's sign ruling? Would the *enragés* of the Bloc Québécois or Parti Québécois or Mouvement Québec français go out of their way to smother the rich and pampered English community of ·Montreal – as they see it – in kindness? One might not see a repeat of St. Bartholemew's Night – the massacre of France's Protestants under Henri III back in 1572 – but the atmosphere might well be that surrounding the revocation of the Edict of Nantes by Louis XIV in 1685, when religious toleration ended. Many of Quebec's anglophones would feel that over two centuries of uninterrupted settlement was coming to an end; like France's Huguenots, they would search for friendly havens, in this case to the west or south.

I am deliberately painting a canvas in sombre colours, if only to underline the risks that face us if ethnic nationalism gets out of hand. There can be no more certain way of ensuring that any Canada-Quebec Union is stillborn, that we embark on our road as two sociological nations as bitter enemies, than through the mistreatment of our respective minorities. Any incident in the one society will be played back – magnified a hundredfold if necessary – in the other. Evidence of intolerance will become justification for retributive intolerance. The spiral would run steadily downwards.

This might seem argument enough to pull back before it is too late, to cobble together some new Meech Lake Accord, whatever the price. I beg to differ. We have crossed a certain divide over the past decades. Quebec sees itself as a sociological nation and will accept no political arrangement that fails to do the same. We in English Canada – whether we like it or not – are obliged to follow suit. There is no putting the old Humpty Dumpty of Canadian federalism together again.

Instead, we must confront the question of minority rights head-on, looking for solutions within the rubric of a two-nation Canada. Officially unilingual societies need not prove intolerant toward their linguistic minorities, just as official bilingualism is no guarantee of minority rights being respected; everything depends on the spirit in which we enter upon the experiment before us.

I wish to argue for a position that, at first blush, seems to fly in the face of nationalism and everything it represents. If nationalism speaks to the concerns of a collectivity with common bonds of language, culture, history, and territory, why should one expect its adherents to show particular tolerance toward minorities? These are linguistically *other*, probably ethnically *other*, communities, articulating values that may be profoundly alien, if not downright threatening, to the majority national group. That majority group may have to pay the price of tolerance in terms of its own homogeneity and cohesiveness. Why go through a long struggle for national self-affirmation if only to throw it all away by accepting limitations on what the linguistic majority can finally undertake?

Self-limiting nationalism sounds a lot less exhilarating than the nationalism of ethnic solidarity or messianic liberation. It seems to speak to the head, rather than the heart, and makes light of the expressive dreams that a romantic form of nationalism embodies. Can one really expect Québécois, who in their hundreds of thousands celebrated the post-Meech St. Jean Baptiste Day as a sort of secular mass to a French Quebec, to show restraint in their new-found status? Can English Canadians, more phlegmatic though they may be, refrain from taking out on their francophone minority some of the resentment they will now feel toward Quebec?

Just as state sovereignty has come to mean a lot less at the end of the twentieth century than in an earlier period, so it may just be that we are about to usher in nationalisms of a more sober sort. This may sound like wishful thinking at a time when communal tensions run rife through many regions of the globe. Yet the experience with independence in Africa, Asia, and Latin America has shown what a hangover unrestrained nationalism can produce. In the Western world, nationalist passions run less deep than before; two world wars have taught Western Europe, in particular, some of the dangers that come with it.

To a noticeable degree, the political climate at the end of the twentieth century is less ideologically charged than in, say, the 1930s or 1950s. Nationalists may, therefore, be able to put some water into their nationalist wine. People cannot eat or drink or exude nationalism every moment of their waking lives. They cannot afford the economic autarchy that slamming the door to the outside world – or to the society beside them – would entail. They have reasons to be highly suspicious of states that, in the name of nationalism or any other ideology, permit widespread violations of human rights or impose artificial conformity on their citizens. In English Canada and Quebec, we are children of the West, of the Enlightenment, of the liberal revolutions, of an evolving democratic credo, which cannot be wished away. That credo suggests some real limits to what states and nations do.

It will be incumbent on the two respective majorities in the Canada-Quebec Union I envisage to show themselves duly cognisant of this principle. The main reason for this need be neither selfless altruism nor love of humanity in the abstract, though a touch of each will not hurt. There is, in fact, a strong element of self-interest in following such a course. If we have genuine concern for the lot of our fellow language speakers in the territory of our neighbour, we would do well to show openness toward our own linguistic minority; mistreatment will beget mistreatment. A second and even more compelling reason for toleration lies in the consequence for relations between English Canada and Quebec in its absence. How can one expect intimate economic ties, and significant political links to boot, if either society, or both, is riding roughshod over its linguistic minority? The strain would destroy all possibility of collaboration for generations to come. Extremists on either side might welcome such a scenario; it will be for the much larger majorities to ensure they do not get their way. Then there is the question of international opinion. We have seen as recently as this summer what the intemperate actions of the Sûreté du Québec at Oka have done for Quebec's image as regards treatment of its native people. Nor has the burning of effigies of natives by south shore commuters near Montreal helped. If either Quebec or English Canada wishes to indulge in practices that violate widely held norms of civilized behaviour, it will do so at its peril.

Self-limiting nationalism means that each of our two societies, while clearly expressing the shared sentiments of its linguistic majority, does not shut its door to the rights of minorities to live and work and educate their children in their own language. It means that in the charters or bills of rights that English Canada and Quebec establish, minority rights are clearly entrenched. Reciprocal provisions along these lines might even be negotiated between the constituent assemblies of English Canada and Quebec. What is at stake is a non-exclusionary and ultimately non-ethnic definition of nationalism, one that takes the principles of pluralism to heart.

Federal arrangements, if Pierre Elliott Trudeau is to be believed, are the surest way to bring this about. But perhaps we can look just as hopefully to each of our two sociological nations to practise principles of toleration of its own free will. A Quebec that has ceased to be a province like the others and that has made good its claim to be the political homeland of most French Canadians may have reason to be less defensive vis-à-vis its anglophone minority than before. And that minority – those that decide to stay in Quebec or move there in the future – will know full well what the rules of the game are, both in terms of the predominance of French and of the acceptance by francophones of minority anglophone rights. The same will hold true for the francophones of English Canada. Nor is the principle of minority rights limited to our two main linguistic groups. Aboriginal peoples will have to know and feel that they are as integrally respected by Quebec society as by English Canadian; neither one of us should pretend that racism has been absent or injustices not committed in our past. Allophones in Quebec, multicultural groups in English Canada, also need recognition. How we deal with such questions will determine whether our nationalisms are of the open and tolerant variety or of the closed.

Self-limiting nationalism carries further implications. It means that we do not put all our eggs into the nationalist basket and forget the other values by which we live or ought to live. Justice, liberty, equality, and principles of economic distribution need not take second place, even if there remain real and deep divisions within national societies, as between right and left for example, over precisely what these principles mean and how they should be furthered. Similarly, one can accept the legitimacy of nationalism for what it contributes to a sense of community, a sense of rootedness in the modern world. But we can not forget that we have obligations to our fellow human beings, wherever they may be, and to a planet whose very survival is threatened. To be good citizens of national societies, more and more, we must also be good citizens of the world.

Let me then reiterate my strong belief that recognition of minority rights is absolutely crucial if a new confederal arrangement between English Canada and Quebec is to ever get off the ground. We can draw up all the paper documents we want, divide up powers between the Union and the governments of English Canada and Quebec to our heart's content, but if there are signs, even before we set out on such a course, that nationalism will take an ugly form, that minorities will be made to feel they have no place in a Quebec or English Canada where unilingualism becomes a persecuting creed, then all will be lost. Anglophones and francophones alike, English Canadians no less than Québécois, nationalists most of all, must not allow ethnic and linguistic intolerance to take hold.

10

A Canada-Quebec Union

What has been occurring in Canada over the recent period is in no way unique. Multinational federations in general are faced with new challenges at the end of the twentieth century. The trend, unlike what may have been the case in the nineteenth or early twentieth centuries, is away from centralization, as constituent nationalities seek greater autonomy than ever before. The Soviet Union is falling apart at a dizzying speed, with republics from giant Russia to tiny Armenia clawing back power from the centre. Yugoslavia is another federation that will not survive the 1990s in its present form; if it does not disintegrate into five or six pieces, it will instead become a much looser confederation in which Slovenia and Croatia have only vestigial ties to a central government in Belgrade. Czechoslovakia, freed from forty years of one-party rule, has already changed its name to the Federated Republic of Czechs and Slovaks; informed observers expect each of these republics to become a power unto itself, sharing only those functions, such as foreign affairs, defence, and trade, that external contingencies make necessary. India may have come through the Punjab's insurgency intact, but there is no guarantee the centre will not have to yield a good deal more power to the states in the future.

Canada was created at a moment when the nation-state was on the ascendant, when the examples of Britain and France, Germany, and Italy were the norms to be emulated by other nations, large or small, aspiring to a place in the international system. The nation-state continues to be the cornerstone of our twentieth-century world and of such organizations as the United Nations; yet somehow it appears a less convincing unit, less powerful and all-encompassing than before. Economic actors and technological forces within the capitalist world are increasingly global; the mass media spill across borders; sports, theatre, dance, novels, music – from classical to rock – reflect a growing internationalization of cultural forms. Politically as well, the trend is toward greater, not lesser, integration within Europe, North America, Latin America, and East Asia and toward common features across the old ideological and geopolitical divides. Can a closed-box model of the nation-state, inherited from the European past, come through such upheavals unalloyed?

The answer is clearly no. Where this country is concerned, these global transformations have gone hand in hand with new internal strains, chipping away at the nation-state from within. The most dramatic of these, of course, has been Quebec nationalism, which shed its clerical and traditional garb thirty years ago for more modernizing forms. Aboriginal peoples have also experienced powerful nationalist impulses; their calls for self-government, even sovereignty, are ones that the existing structures can scarcely contain. Among English-speaking Canadians, the sense of nationhood is a good deal less ethnic than in the days when Canada's destiny was intimately linked to Britain's. This new Canadianism continues to stress the need for critical distance from the United States. Whether it requires Quebec as a constituent part of its identity and, with it, the maintenance of existing federal structures, is the question we now confront.

It is my contention that we must begin to move away from a one-Canada model, based on the notion of a single Canadian nationality, to something more dualistic, even pluralistic, in character. If Quebec sees itself more and more as sociologically distinct (and our aboriginal peoples make similar claims), English Canadians, particularly in the post-Meech era, may undergo a similar transformation. We will become, for all practical purposes, Canadians with the Québécois removed.

Not entirely removed, mind you. What I have also been arguing is that there is more binding English Canada to Quebec than the simplistic advocates of sovereignty on either side, but especially in Quebec, seem willing to acknowledge. Economic ties speak for themselves and could only be sundered at great cost to both peoples; ordinary Québécois would find a separate currency, in no way tied to the Canadian dollar, a sobering price to pay for Quebec sovereignty. But pay it they would have to, for English Canada would not be prepared to commit its collective resources to shore up a Quebec determined to go its sovereign way. The geopolitical reality of the United States would also confront the advocates of a sovereign Quebec. They might think that language and culture were some sort of shield against American influence, that Quebec could chart an independent course in social programs or industrial policy without suffering the consequences, or that it could conduct foreign or defence policies of its own, but they would be in for a rude awakening. It would be a daunting task for them to deal with the United States all by themselves. They could not then turn to an English Canada they considered their ancestral enemy for help, a society that they had, moreover, alienated through a messy and rancorous separation.

English Canada has much to lose as well if Quebec goes its separate way. It has its own regionalist currents to worry about. Provincial premiers, especially in the West, are more than ready to carve up the federal state. A majority of English Canadians will oppose them, but ongoing links with Quebec in a number of key areas would reinforce the position of the centre and lessen tendencies to balkanization.

Then there is our own relationship with the United States. English Canadian nationalists may delude themselves with the hope that we will continue to hold our own, no less successfully than before, against the American presence. The fact remains that two sovereign states in the northern part of North America in place of one weakens our ability (no less than Quebec's) to fend off the American giant. We have not shown enormous prowess, even as a united country, in resisting economic or cultural domination. Will we fare better with English Canada and Quebec at each other's throats and with our provinces falling over one another in the rush to placate American interests? Finally, there is a territorial element involved, the physical separation between the Atlantic provinces and the rest of Canada that would result from the establishment of a sovereign Quebec between the two. Land and air links could be maintained, or in the event of glacial relations with Quebec, replaced by air or land links through the northeastern United States. But the sentiment in English Canada would be that of a ruptured country, which might well hasten the disintegration of what remained.

We need an alternative that better suits the needs both of English Canadians and Québécois. The federal arrangements of 1867 have had their day, and attempts to postpone the hour of reckoning, through the Official Languages Act or the Meech Lake Accord, have failed. Quebec wants to radically rearrange the shared living space on the basis of two sociological nations rather than one. The analogy one might make is to a couple, where one of the partners desires a condominium arrangement instead of a common household. They may still be living in the same contiguous space and share common expenses (e.g., heat, light, mortgage payments, and taxes) as well as a common property line with the neighbour, but each partner will be out of the other's kitchen, living room, and bedroom. Each will have much greater autonomy than before.

This is what a Canada-Quebec Union boils down to. It replaces the joint Canada household established in 1867 with a condominium-type arrangement. Quebec becomes quite distinct from English Canada; it is no longer a province sending members to the Canadian Parliament; most of Ottawa's powers have reverted to it; it is largely master in its own home. English Canada proceeds to establish a government of its own; Quebec can no longer stymie Senate reform; we can give our federal government a more or less significant role over culture, higher education, or social affairs, as we see fit; we can, if we choose, give primacy to Charter rights over ordinary legislative acts; English Canada is free to be itself.

Yet neither Quebec nor English Canada is fully sovereign. We accept the fact that there are constraints – particularly external – that make it important to preserve a common framework. We have more to gain than to lose in terms of influence in international affairs – within the OECD, the IMF, the World Bank, GATT, the UN, and NATO – as members of a single unit. We significantly increase our bargaining position with the United States and our ability to retain those elements of culture or social policy or economic strategy that make us distinctive. We acknowledge that a common currency is the backbone of any ongoing economic union, that environmental problems span our borders, that common citizenship will continue to link our two peoples.

I am not the only one to advocate such a scheme. In the late 1970s, Gérard Bergeron, a Laval political scientist, called for a Canadian commonwealth in a series of articles in *Le Devoir*.* The gist of his proposal was fairly similar to what I have in mind: a two-nation arrangement, with a fair degree of autonomy for each but with certain vital links between them. Some of the musings out of Quebec in recent months, in particular Robert Bourassa's allusion to a superstructural arrangement between Quebec and English Canada along the lines of the European Community, strike an analogous chord. Writers like Georges Mathews or Pierre Fournier echo the theme.† So perhaps this essay gives expression to a responding voice from English Canada.

* These were reprinted in *Le Devoir*, 28, 29 June, 1990.
† Georges Mathews, "New Deal from Quebec: A Canadian Community," *Globe and Mail*, 22 May 1990, A7; Pierre Fournier, *Autopsie du Lac Meech: La Souveraineté est-elle inévitable?*, Montréal, VLB, 1990.

A chart – my one concession to the games political scientists play – might be in order at this point. It outlines the structures of the proposed Canada-Quebec Union and some of the powers to be vested in it.

The Canada-Quebec Union

Government of the Canada-Quebec Union
(foreign policy, defence, international trade, finance,
including a common bank, environment, citizenship)

Parliament of the Canada-Quebec Union

Government of English Canada   Government of Quebec

Parliament of English Canada

Elected House   Elected Senate   Elected Quebec   The National
of Commons   delegates to the Assembly
                                        Canada-Quebec
                                        Union

Governments of the Nine
Provinces and Two Territories

Elected Legislatures

For those who like historical analogies, this might be called the Austro-Hungarian solution to Canada's dilemma. The year of Canadian Confederation, 1867, was also the year in which the Hapsburg Empire was restructured into a dual monarchy between Austria and Hungary. Each component acquired complete control over internal affairs; foreign policy, the armed forces, and tariffs came under a common imperial rubric. This rear-

92

rangement brought an end to much of the discord between Austrians and Hungarians that had been tearing the Empire apart; it did not, however, satisfy the other nationalities – Poles, Czechs, Slovaks, Rumanians, Slovenians, Croatians – who only achieved their emancipation after the First World War. (Aboriginal people take note!) The remaking of the Hapsburg Empire, moreover, was very much an initiative carried out from above; only the aristocratic elites of Vienna and Budapest were involved. We clearly will have to do things differently in the Canada of the 1990s.

I see the process of moving toward a Canada-Quebec Union as tremendously empowering, a means of allowing the people of English Canada and Quebec – first generation or tenth, aboriginal or post-European settlement – a real say in the type of political arrangements by which we wish to be governed. I cannot, for one moment, conceive of our going down this road without far-ranging political debate and the use of democratic procedures like constituent assemblies and referenda. For once in the history of Canada, our political elites will not be imposing constitutional arrangements over our heads.

If the peoples of Eastern Europe or Latin America or East Asia can try take charge of their own destinies and rewrite their histories in a more democratic vein, why should we fear to do the same? If multinational federations have ceased to satisfy one or the other of their constituent nationalities, why should we rule out a looser confederal arrangement in their stead? Nothing will come easily – or without risk – in the brave new Canada that lies ahead. Aboriginal rights need to be dealt with fairly by both of our societies; linguistic minorities must be assured they will not become sacrificial lambs; nationalism – whether English Canadian or Québécois – must be self-limiting; there must be a mutual desire to make the Canada-Quebec structures work.

Still, I am convinced that something like the model I have sketched will come to be. I do not think that Canada will simply fall apart, despite the predictions of gloom and doom emanating from Brian Mulroney and the chorus of Meech Lake boosters in June 1990. Nor need English Canada and Quebec be turned into inveterate enemies staring each other down across the Ottawa River. I do not think we will make a mockery of minority rights or aboriginal rights or principles like toleration and mutual respect in our dealings with one another. And I think we will learn the virtues of active citizenship that come from long and deep reflection on the fate of one's country. So there is life after Meech – a better life, if we arrange things properly, for both English Canadians and Québécois, than would have been possible with it. Ours may be the first generation to create something quite original in the history of two nations living side by side. Is it too soon to propose a toast to a future Canada-Quebec Union?